The Breakthrough of Kampfgruppe Peiper in the Battle of the Bulge

The Breakthrough of Kampfgruppe Peiper in the Battle of the Bulge

Hugues Wenkin and Christian Dujardin

Pen & Sword
MILITARY

First published in Great Britain in 2024 by
Pen & Sword Military
An imprint of Pen & Sword Books Limited
Yorkshire – Philadelphia

ISBN 978 1 03610 403 0

A CIP catalogue record for this book is available from the British Library

Typeset by Mac Style
Printed in the UK by CPI Group (UK) Ltd, Croydon, CR0 4YY.

MIX
Paper | Supporting responsible forestry
FSC® C013604

Pen & Sword Books Limited incorporates the imprints of After the Battle, Atlas, Archaeology, Aviation, Discovery, Family History, Fiction, History, Maritime, Military, Military Classics, Politics, Select, Transport, True Crime, Air World, Frontline Publishing, Leo Cooper, Remember When, Seaforth Publishing, The Praetorian Press, Wharncliffe Local History, Wharncliffe Transport, Wharncliffe True Crime and White Owl.

For a complete list of Pen & Sword titles please contact

PEN & SWORD BOOKS LIMITED
47 Church Street, Barnsley, South Yorkshire, S70 2AS, England
E-mail: enquiries@pen-and-sword.co.uk
Website: www.pen-and-sword.co.uk
or
PEN AND SWORD BOOKS
1950 Lawrence Rd, Havertown, PA 19083, USA
E-mail: uspen-and-sword@casematepublishers.com
Website: www.penandswordbooks.com

'Der Teufel steckt im Detail.'
(The devil is in the detail)
Friedrich Nietzsche

Contents

Introduction

Our first encounter with Kampfgruppe (KG) Peiper was in 2006. I [Hugues Wenkin] was writing articles for the French military magazine *Batailles et Blindés* as an amateur historian. At that time, Christian Dujardin and I were working on the same team, and when he heard that I was writing an article on KG Peiper, he generously made himself available to guide me. He was already passionate about the subject and my visit to La Gleize was the starting point of a fruitful collaboration that has since developed into a strong friendship.

At the time, the first results of our joint research only amounted to a few pages. The more you know, however, the more you find out that you know nothing; a miracle of

'Führer command, we will follow you.' This slogan perfectly sums up the main idea of the offensive. (*NARA*)

science that has always amazed me. From discussion to discussion, the list of questions about this Kampfgruppe grew and grew. Each question was followed by a research project and often by a publication in one form or other.

The idea for this book came from the desire to bring all our work together. After a day of looking through our various articles on the subject, we realised that we would need at least four volumes to cover everything.

Let me reassure you that this first volume is not just a series of copy and pastes. The old articles have been copiously revisited. It must be said that between the time of their initial writing and the time of their re-use, a lot of water has flowed along the River Amblève. Our archives have been enriched, our methods have been professionalised, and many volumes by other authors have been acquired. This additional information has enabled us to answer questions that had previously been left unanswered, while at the same time raising new questions.

The historian knows that it is impossible for them to touch the truth with their fingers; they know that they can only reconstruct elements like a puzzle. Many pieces of evidence have disappeared since the events. Papers have been burned, witnesses have died, publications have been left in dusty boxes. We have unearthed a great deal, but we remain convinced that there is still much to discover.

Hugues Wenkin and Christian Dujardin

Chapter 1

The German Plan

Between Dreams and Strategic Options

During the summer of 1944, the Wehrmacht was pushed back to the borders of Germany. The front stabilised in September, however, when the Allied offensive ran out of steam after having stretched its lines of communication to the limit. On the Western Front, the Third Reich still controlled half of the Netherlands and the north-east of France. Belgium had been completely liberated. In fact, the American divisions on their way to Germany had come up against the defensive positions of the Siegfried Line (Westwall), which were rehabilitated in record time.

Since 1939, the Allies had trumpeted the fact that they would hang their laundry on the Siegfried Line. They had to wait five long years to do so. (*NARA*)

The Westwall remained an effective barrier. (*NARA*)

Despite its immense losses in battle, Germany still had nearly 10 million men under arms, with 7.5 million in the army and its other ground force, the Nazi Party's praetorian guard, the Waffen-SS.

Yet there were still many others who could be sent into battle: previously exempted students, men with one physical disability or another, non-essential civil servants, convalescents coming out of hospital, sailors without ships and airmen without planes who were transformed, by force of circumstance, into infantrymen, and new classes that were made available for conscription by simply extending the age limits downwards and upwards (between 16 and 60 years of age).

Moreover, there was no question of the rear guard collapsing. The sinister *Geheime Staatspolizei* (Gestapo) eliminated the internal threat of the Communists – or at least drove it underground – so that during the war years no significant popular protest could take place at all. The reprobate officers who were involved in the 20 July plot to kill Hitler were executed so mercilessly – those deemed most involved were hanged by butcher's hooks while their agony was filmed for posterity – that there was no fear of renewed opposition. On the contrary, the Nazi's grip on Germany had never been stronger. On the other hand, the aerial bombardments and the demand for unconditional surrender strengthened the will of the German people. More than ever, Reichsminister Joseph Goebbels brandished the threat of unconditional surrender to all Germans to galvanise the civilian population. As Hasso Eccard von Manteuffel[1] later put it:

> *And this... 'thanks' to Roosevelt who, in January 1943, during a press conference, had announced the Allies' willingness to force Germany into unconditional surrender. Big mistake!*
>
> *Then, in September 1944, the Morgenthau Plan was published. This plan, as you will recall, was to lead to the conversion of Germany into a predominantly agricultural and pastoral country and the dismantling of all its factories. These were two of many gross errors that prolonged the war and drove the German military, from the private to the general – the highest ranking – to despair. All decided to defend the Fatherland to the last breath, and the GIs would know the cost of being opposed to an adversary whose strength is increased tenfold by this conviction, this certainty:* Una salus victis, nullam sperare salutem.[2]

With the benefit of historical hindsight, it is sometimes difficult to get into the heads of the leaders of the time. No one better than Hitler himself can explain the reasons why he gambled his final offensive reserve in a huge roll of the dice. On 11 and 12 December 1944, only four days before the start of the operation, he summoned together all the general officers concerned, up to the level of divisional commanders, who had been kept in total ignorance until then. He then explained to them the military and strategic-political aims of the planned offensive:

Goebbels' propaganda used the Morgenthau Plan to galvanise the resistance of the German people. (*NARA*)

> *War is obviously a severe test for all those involved. The longer it lasts, the more painful this ordeal becomes. This hardship must be endured as long as there is any hope of success. When hopes of victory fade, the hardships are usually no longer endured with the same will as, for example, that with which a fortress fights as long as it can still hope to lift the siege it is under. It is therefore important to remove the enemy's confidence in his victory from time to time, by making him understand by offensive blows that the success of his plans cannot be expected with certainty. This can never be achieved as well by successful defensive action as by successful offensive action. We cannot, therefore, in the long run, hold to the principle that defence is the strongest form of combat* [...] *We must not forget that the total number of men engaged on our side is still as high as on our opponent's side. We must not lose sight of the fact that part of the enemy's forces is fixed in East Asia against Japan, against a state which, without China, numbers well over 100 million men and which constitutes an important factor in terms of technical equipment. It must be realised, however, that too long periods of purely defensive resistance will eat away in the long run, and that they must in any case be followed by victorious battles.*

Hitler went on to set out his views on the political effect that a victory was likely to have on the opposing coalition:

> *One thing more to think about, gentlemen. Never in the whole history of the world has there been a coalition of such heterogeneous elements and of such divergent aims as that*

Hitler issued his plans to the officers concerned. (*NARA*)

> *of our opponents. The opponents we face today are the greatest extremes to be found on earth: on the one hand, ultra-capitalist states, on the other, ultra-Marxist states; on the one hand, an expiring world empire, Great Britain, on the other, a colony in search of a legacy, the United States. These are states whose goals are in conflict with each other day after day. And anyone who, like a spider in the centre of its web, I might say, observes this development can see that this antagonism is growing by the hour. If we can still deal them a few heavy blows it may happen at any moment that this artificially maintained common front collapses with a thunderous noise. Each of the partners has entered this coalition with the hope of being able to achieve its political objectives [...] of being able to fool the others or of being able to take advantage of them: the United States is trying to inherit England, Russia is trying to conquer the Balkans, to conquer the Straits, to conquer the oil of Persia, Iran, the Persian Gulf; England is trying to maintain its position and to strengthen the position it occupies in the Mediterranean. In other words, the day will come and it could happen now at any moment, because on the other side, too, history is shaped by mortal men. The day will come when this coalition will unravel, always on condition that under no circumstances will this struggle give rise to a moment of weakness on the part of Germany.*[3]

In addition, on the Western Front the Allied armies threatened a region vital to Germany's industry: the Ruhr. Hitler took up the adage of von Schlieffen, the architect of

Generalfeldmarschall Von Rundstedt (second from left) did not believe the offensive in the Ardennes would be a success. In the background, Dönitz, Keitel and Guderian can be seen in discussion. (*NARA*)

The fighting raged in the Hürtgen Forest: the Americans would remain there until February 1945. (*NARA*)

the August 1914 plan of operations, who said: '*Better the enemy in East Prussia than on the Rhine.*' Despite their strategic advantage, however, the Allies had lines of communication that were too long. In addition, there were the fortifications on the western border, the Westwall, which combined concrete anti-tank barriers (the famous dragon's teeth) and bunkers. No matter how outdated this pre-war system was, Hitler was convinced that concrete made defences easier. Moreover, the wooded and hilly terrain along the border was difficult to approach. The bloody battles in the Hürtgen Forest confirmed this assumption. In the west, too, Germany could expect a short respite while Dwight David Eisenhower prepared his final assault.

There was no hope of striking a politically decisive blow in the east. The number of new and re-equipped divisions Hitler had at his disposal would simply be swallowed up in a fight to the death with the Red Army, without obtaining a result that could change the course of events. In the west, however, the situation was different. The distances to a strategic objective were shorter, and as we have seen above, the potential for a victory on this side could have a decisive effect on the situation. It is therefore in the west that Germany needed to play its final card.

In short, the Führer's idea was to strike a decisive blow to Anglo-American morale and get them to break away from what he considered an unnatural alliance with the Soviets. He also rightly believed that the overly defensive option would only continue to erode

Generalfeldmarschall Walter Model (seen here shaking hands with Hitler) had the heavy responsibility of commanding the entire offensive. (*NARA*)

the German military potential and, ultimately, lead to an inevitable defeat. There was only one option left: a sufficiently strong and violent attack to make an impression and throw the opponent off its guard.

It was on the basis of these geostrategic considerations that operation *Wacht am Rhein* was launched. Heeresgruppe B, under the command of Generalfeldmarschall Walter Model, was given the delicate task of leading the offensive. Two armoured armies were reconstituted for this purpose.

The Genesis of a Plan

At the end of summer 1944, when the Allied armies were forced to take a break due to a lack of supplies, Adolf Hitler decided to take the initiative on the Western Front. The first idea that germinated in the offices of the OKW (Oberkommando der Wehrmacht)[4] was to use Heeresgruppe G, under the orders of Generaloberst Johannes Blaskowitz, to strike Patton's Third Army in its rear. The operation was aborted to make way for a much more grandiose project.

Around 25 September, Generaloberst Jodl, head of the OKW, was instructed to begin a detailed feasibility analysis of an operation whose main principles were imposed on him by the dictator. The latter had just recovered from jaundice and seemed to have used his convalescence to think about the operation. The attack should be launched between 20 and 30 November, consisting of a breakthrough through the Ardennes in the Monschau-Echternach sector to cross the River Meuse between Namur and Liège, to capture the city of Antwerp, in particular its port infrastructures, in order to prevent the delivery of supplies and reinforcements to the Allied armies. If the operation was successful, it would also isolate Montgomery's 21st Army Group in the north from the rest of the Allied forces. The Führer's strategic goals were in line with his political intentions. If he succeeded, he could condemn Churchill's soldiers fighting in Holland to a new Dunkirk. The result would be a battle to annihilate the Anglo-Canadian forces north of the Antwerp-Liège-Bastogne line, which could potentially shatter the coalition already weakened by the bitter failure at Arnhem. The psychological blow of this would likely destroy the morale of the British population definitively and force Britain to make a separate peace, leaving the American army alone to face the Wehrmacht. The United States would, in turn, be forced to let go of Europe. Hitler could then force both countries to surrender and thus obtain the signing of a separate peace agreement on the Western Front by banking on the ideological rift between Roosevelt, Churchill and Stalin. The German army could then be transferred to the Eastern Front to stop the advance of the Soviet Red Army.

Jodl thought Antwerp was reachable, but doubted the possibility of breaking up Montgomery's armies.[5] He had to assume that at least thirty divisions would be

Germany could expect some respite in the West while Eisenhower prepared his final assault. (*NAC*)

available, ten of them armoured, and that considerable support would be provided by an unprecedented concentration of artillery and rocket launchers.

Operational control would be ensured by a total of four armies: two armoured to form the spearhead and two infantry to cover the northern and southern flanks. The Luftwaffe would need to be prepared to support the operation, and the planning would particularly aim to preserve tactical surprise by focusing on speed of execution. The note ends by stressing the importance of secrecy and indeed, a very limited number of participants would be involved in the development of the battle plan.

The staff went into action and finally proposed five scenarios:

- An attack in the form of a single thrust launched from Venlo and aimed at Antwerp.
- A two-pronged offensive, with the main effort starting from Luxembourg and moving northwards, and a secondary axis heading southwards from the north-western sector of Aachen.
- A project also materialised by two pincer movements launched simultaneously from Luxembourg and Metz to seize Longwy.
- An operation in Lorraine consisting of a double envelopment, planned from Metz and Baccarat to converge on Nancy.
- An envelopment carried out in two thrusts, one starting from the east of Épinal and the other from the east of Montbéliard, the junction point being made in the Vesoul sector.[6]

Only the SS had the Führer's confidence after the attack of 20 July 1944. SS-Oberstgruppenführer Sepp Dietrich (third from left, seen decorating the SS combatant) would be the flag bearer of Himmler's Waffen-SS in the upcoming battle. (*NARA*)

Of these five options, the staff recommended the first two. The Dutch option was considered risky, but at the same time it was the most promising from a strategic point of view. While the Liège-Aachen operation offered the possibility of annihilating a large part of the enemy troops in the Aachen salient. Hitler accepted both recommended solutions and ordered the study of a new plan synthesising the two. The concept of a double envelopment with the two pincers of the attack starting from two distant areas to form a large cauldron particularly caught his attention. This solution entered the dialectic of the offensive under the name '*die grosse Lösung*'.[7] However, it appeared to the staff that this option was not in line with the available means. Without the support of the field commanders, Jodl did not dare oppose the Führer's proposal. Discussions focused on the location of the southern border of the planned operation. Hitler had a broad view and envisaged the Wasserbillig–Arlon line and the north bank of the Semois. The OKW's proposal was much more modest, suggesting a southern limit at Diekirch, passing north of Martelange towards Neufchâteau.

Work of the General Staff

Ten days after the initial presentation, Jodl returned to Hitler to present his order of deployment (*Aufmarschanweisung*). In German practice, this term refers to a directive containing the basis of a plan to be used for the development of a practical subject. Normally, this second part of the work was undertaken by the Stab, who would, in fact, direct the planned operation. So, even before Hitler gave his final approval to the proposal, on 22 October the chiefs of staff concerned were summoned to the Wolf's Lair, the command post located in East Prussia. General der Kavallerie Siegfried Westphal, of OB WEST, and General der Infanterie Hans Krebs of Walter Model's Heeresgruppe B were present. They had to sign a document binding them to the secrecy of a mysterious operation called *Wacht am Rhein,* a name chosen in part to confuse potential spies by giving the impression that the project was to prepare a better defence of the river flowing through Cologne. Another name was used to cover the instructions with the seal of secrecy, with the added advantage that it could be used to give instructions about the defence of Aachen: *Abwehrschlacht im Westen.*

After a first conference, the two officers were invited to a second one in a smaller committee in the presence of the Führer. The latter revealed to them the plans for an operation intended to encircle and destroy all American and British forces north of a line between Bastogne and Brussels–Antwerp. It was to be carried out in two phases: the first consisted of crossing the Meuse and the second of driving towards Antwerp to carry out a large-scale envelopment of the Allied position to the north. Heeresgruppe B would have three armies to meet this objective: the 5. and 6. Panzer-Armee would be in the front line, while the 7. Armee in the south would protect the left wing from the assault.

Two deadlines were set: 20 November, which determined the end of preparations for an attack, and 25 November, the day of the attack itself. This timeframe was chosen by the director of the Luftwaffe's meteorological service, Doctor Schuster, who proposed

The leading units were supported by five Flak regiments, twelve Volks-Artillerie-Korps and ten Nebelwerfer-Brigaden. (*Rights reserved*)

it in response to Hitler's wish to have ten days of overcast weather to ground the Allied air force in order to prevent its irremediable control of the skies from hampering ground movements. Moreover, 25 November corresponded to a new moon, darkening the sky so as to reduce the effectiveness of the night bombing. It should be noted that from the outset Jodl doubted the feasibility of launching the attack on this date, as planning the arrival of reinforcements required much more time than the dictator imagined. Moreover, not only was the weather overcast, but the ground also had to be free of water and stable enough to support the armoured traffic. In this respect, the second half of December, with its night frosts, was more favourable.

The two officers were informed that they would be able to count on eighteen Infanteriedivisionen and twelve mechanised divisions, the whole being supported by the following: five Flak regiments, twelve Volks-Artillerie-Korps, and ten Nebelwerfer-Brigaden. Faced with the scepticism of the two generals, Hitler gave his word that the Luftwaffe would support the operation with 2,000 fighters, of which 100 would be jets. Generalfeldmarschall Wilhelm Keitel gave his officer's word that 16 million litres of fuel would be available for the day of the attack and that fifty trains of ammunition would be in reserve. On this point, Jodl would claim after the war that the figures quoted by Keitel were extravagant. For example, only thirty trains were actually available, each carrying 500 tonnes. General der Kavallerie Siegfried Westphal wrote a report for Von Rundstedt, his superior, about Hitler's intentions and concluded:

> *I am glad that at least we will receive more forces in the west. Before this offensive begins, a lot of water will flow into the Rhine. From a preliminary point of view I can say that the objective of Antwerp cannot be achieved with the means available because the long flanks to be defended on both sides are threatened by two attacks and there are not enough divisions available to cover them. Even if Model could push forward as far as the Meuse, the result would be a salient front coming out to the west, holding it will require a lot of manpower and potentially invite a flanking assault from the enemy. I am of the opinion that a less ambitious objective should be found in which strong enemy forces could be destroyed without great risk. The whole plan of this offensive return seems to me to be totally unrealistic.*[8]

Generalfeldmarschall Von Rundstedt immediately agreed with his chief of staff's diagnosis of the plan's weaknesses but went even further. In his eyes, the very preparation of the attack was potentially dangerous, as it was inevitable that the units participating in the initiative would have to be withdrawn from the front. This would create a danger on the flanks, possibly giving the Allies the opportunity to prevent the operation by an attempt on their part against the weakened sectors. At best, he felt, the end result of Hitler's plan would be the creation of a huge salient in the style of those obtained during the First World War, swallowing up a good portion of the available reserves. He therefore advocated a more moderate solution, aiming to strike in the Liège area in order to achieve a tactical victory that would weaken the Allies through the heavy losses caused. He was joined on this point of view by Model, who in particular envisaged an attack in the Aachen sector, which he considered to be highly threatened. The idea that germinated in the heads of the generals was to provide another project that would please the Führer and be easier to implement.

Hitler decided to entrust his armoured spearhead, the 6. Panzer-Armee, to Sepp Dietrich, one of his oldest supporters. (*NARA*)

Two plans were finally presented at a conference held on 27 October in Fichtenhain. On this occasion, the commanders chosen to lead the two Panzer-Armeen were invited. They were General der Panzertruppen Hasso Eccard von Manteuffel and SS-Oberstgruppenführer Josef 'Sepp' Dietrich. General der Panzertruppen Erich Brandenberger joined them as commander of the 7. Armee. The instruction he received began: '*The objective of the operation is to achieve a change in the entire campaign in the west and, perhaps, in the entire war by annihilating the enemy forces north of the Antwerp-Brussels-Luxembourg line.*' Hitler went on to say, '*I have the firm resolution to insist, at all times, on the execution of the operation, even if the enemy's attack on both sides of Metz and the forthcoming assault on the Ruhr district should result in great losses of ground and positions.*'[9]

The precision of the definition of the German device under Model's orders is refined. The 6. Panzer-Armee,[10] under the command of SS-Oberstgruppenführer and Panzer Generaloberst der Waffen-SS Sepp Dietrich, was to attack at the level of Liège, travel 90 kilometres to bypass the city of the Moselle by the south and drive towards Antwerp, 110 kilometres further north, the port of Antwerp being the strategic objective of the adventure.

The 5. Panzer-Armee of General der Panzertruppen Hasso Eccard von Manteuffel had to go south via Namur to capture Brussels. Its mission was in fact to protect the

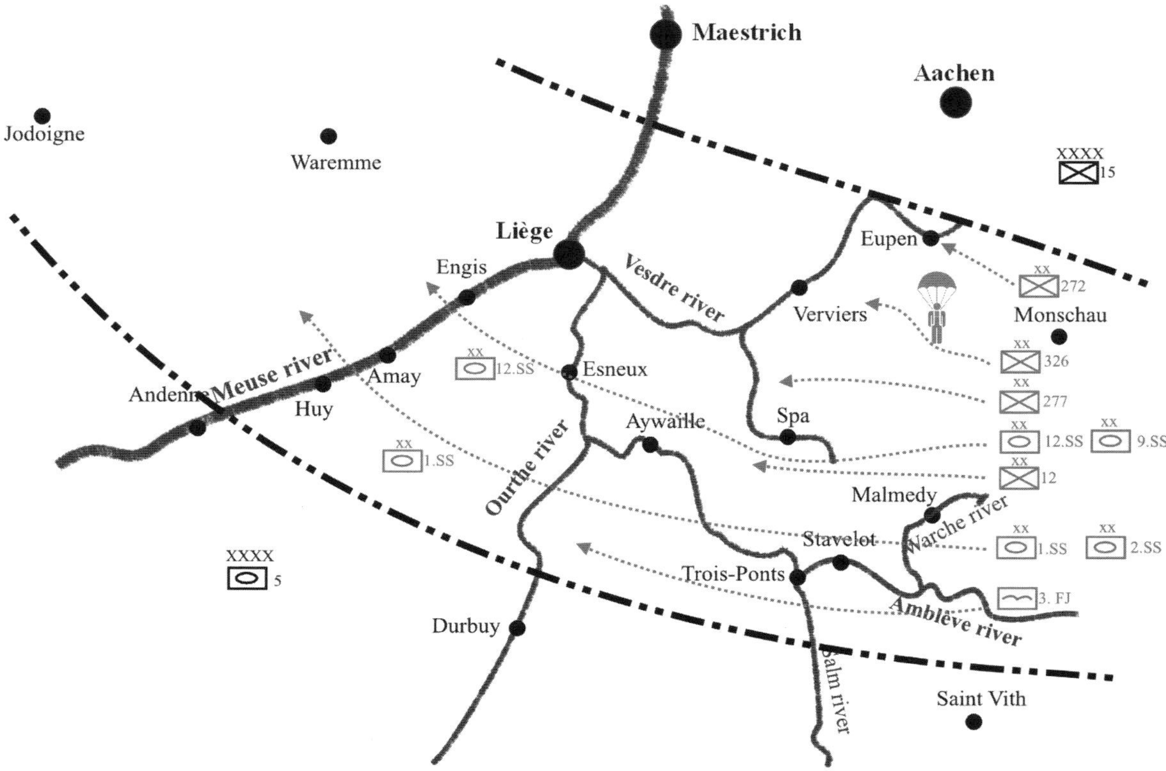

The ambitious plan of the offensive. (*Coll. Authors*)

lines of communication of Dietrich's men. Roads were scarce in the Ardennes, so the protection of the road junctions was absolutely essential for the success of the operation.

Finally, Walter Model also led the 15. Armee of General der Infanterie Gustav-Adolf von Zangen in the north, and was in charge of holding the American forces in the Aachen area in order to avoid a pincer movement of the armoured salient in formation. In the south, the 7. Armee of General der Panzertruppen Erich Brandenberger had to advance due west from Luxembourg to protect the left flank and, above all, to block the main threat to the operation: Patton's Third Army.

The Generals are Doubtful

After the plan was revealed, Von Manteuffel immediately aligned himself with the views of Von Rundstedt and Model. He stated after the war:

> *After the missions were assigned, the allocation of resources was discussed. Generalfeldmarschall Model and I were of the opinion that the distance to the objective was too great. Questioned by Von Rundstedt, I said that I believed my forces were strong enough to reach the Meuse. The next day I discussed the operation plans with*

Generalfeldmarschall Model and his chief of staff, General der Infanterie Krebs. We agreed that, depending on the distribution of troops, a small solution had to be found. We planned to advance the 5. Panzer-Armee to the Meuse and then turn north, and in conjunction with the 6. Panzer-Armee and the 15. Armee, destroy the enemy forces east of the river. If a major solution was ordered, the thrust of the 15. Armee had to be cancelled so that its units could reinforce our two armoured armies. Under no circumstances were the promised material and personnel resources to be reduced, nor were any units to be withdrawn from the 15. and 7. Armee. Sufficient supplies of fuel and ammunition needed to be in the hands of the troops before the attack began. The Panzerdivisionen and Volks-Artillerie-Korps, shattered by the decisive battles at Aachen, had to be reorganised. Air support for the fighting force on the ground and air reconnaissance had to be maintained. Traffic control units belonging to the Todt Organisation needed to be provided to the frontline regiments, because all engineer units would be used for important tasks and the roads would be congested. Unit and staff transmission groups had to be reorganised. I also wanted to have influence on all assignments (this request was immediately guaranteed to me by Hitler).[11]

Von Manteuffel gave a more detailed account of their discussions and the alternative solution in an interview with the historian B.H. Liddell Hart:

We were agreed in our objections to the plan. Firstly, we thought the strategic device was defective, exposing the flanks too much and putting them at risk. Moreover, the ammunition planned was not sufficient to reach such a distant goal. In addition, the superiority of the enemy air force presented a serious obstacle. Finally, we knew that the Allies had large reserves in France and England. I myself stressed the danger posed by the airborne divisions stationed in England, ready to intervene. I added that the quality of the road network beyond the Meuse would facilitate Allied counter-attacks. We sent a report to the OKW stating that the planned offensive was unfeasible with our numbers. At the same time we proposed a modified plan: the 15. Armee, strongly supported on its right wing, would attack north of Aachen, towards Maastricht. The 6. Panzer-Armee would attack south of Aachen and bypass the city to eventually try to establish a bridgehead across the Meuse in the Liège area. The main objective here was to attract Allied attention. The 5. Armee panzers would attack from the Eifel, through the Ardennes, towards Namur, with the mission of creating a bridgehead there. The armies would then all turn inland and envelop the Allied positions along the Meuse. If the opposition weakened, they would exploit their success by advancing on Antwerp, otherwise the damage could be limited.[12]

In view of these analyses, the head of OB West, Generalfeldmarschall Gerd von Rundstedt, fully supported the opinion of these generals and insisted that the smaller solution be adopted. His opinion was rejected by Hitler, despite the fact that he stated it would be impossible to achieve the objectives given the state of the personnel, equipment and supplies.

Model doubted whether Antwerp could be reached, but Volks-Grenadier units were committed en masse. (*Rights reserved*)

The plans continued to be refined, Von Rundstedt, whose name the press would associate with the preparation of the offensive, did not seem to be overly involved in the planning of the assault. At the meeting on 2 December, he was represented by Generalleutnant Siegfried Westphal, to the great astonishment of the leader of the Third Reich. One can understand his lack of involvement in the project when considering the old marshal's point of view:

> *The plan, received in November, amazed me. Hitler had not bothered to consult me about the possibilities of success. It was obvious to me that our numbers were not equal to such an ambitious plan. Model agreed with me. In fact, not a single soldier could believe in the possibility of reaching Antwerp. Alas! I knew what to say about the uselessness of uttering the word 'impossible' in front of Hitler.*

Günther Blumentritt added: '*In reality, the Field Marshal was opposed to any offensive on our part. His intention was to defend the Ruhr and to hold all the armoured divisions in reserve, behind that line, to repel in force any breakthrough from the front. He wanted to apply a defensive strategy.*'[13]

The only significant changes in the proposed plan concern the planned crossing points on the Meuse. Initially, the 6. Panzer-Armee was to cross the river between Liège and Andenne inclusively, while the 5. Panzer-Armee was to cross between Namur and

Andenne. Around 10 December, the bridges were selected by the different Stab within the sectors that concerned them. Von Manteuffel set his sights on the Dinant bridge, although it was outside his initial zone. His stated aim was to increase the number of possible routes in order to increase his chances of overcoming the main obstacle, despite the fact that when he turned north, he would find the River Sambre in his path. Generalleutnant Büchs, a staff officer at the OKW and second deputy to Generaloberst Alfred Jodl, believed that von Manteuffel actually changed his crossing point to be closer to his original plan. He also pointed out that the dictator carefully avoided Liège because of his opposition to the smaller solution and the memory of Stalingrad, where it had proved impossible for an armoured army to cross a large wetland in the immediate vicinity of a large urban centre.

The Chief of Staff of the 6. Panzer-Armee, SS-Brigadenführer Fritz Kraemer, claimed to have been informed of the plan on 16 November:

> *Four major considerations were taken into account in the selection of the sector for the attack. Our forces north of the Ardennes were strong enough to contain a thrust north of Aachen because of our control of the Ruhr dams and the consequent threat of flooding in the Ruhr valley. We had to find where the Americans were weakest. We had to select an area that was favourable for our operations. We needed an area that could help us if the weather turned clear. The Eifel has considerable wooded areas in which we could hide our vehicles if the American Air Force was operational. I was personally very familiar with this territory, as I was Chief of Staff of the I. SS-Pz-Korps during the retreat from France and our assembly area was then around Prüm. For my part, I was in favour of an attack in the Aachen sector for two reasons. The soldiers would have fought better to recover German soil. We would have had little difficulty with the terrain, whereas the Americans would have had to move their forces through an unfavourable area. We would also have had a better chance of destroying enemy troops there than in the Ardennes. However, it is true that the USAF would have had less difficulty in getting us on a clear day.*[14]

A Well-Kept Secret

The secrecy surrounding the Battle of the Bulge was one of the main features of the operation. Hitler demanded that briefed personnel sign a document warning them that if the plans were revealed, the sentence would be death. Jodl mitigated the decree by saying that this was an exaggeration, but that any disclosure, whether intentional or negligent, was punishable by court martial. One of the measures specified that the information was not to be transported by air. The precaution was taken to avoid a repeat of the Mechelen-sur-Meuse affair, where on 10 January 1940, plans for the invasion intended for the following week fell into the hands of Belgian intelligence after a navigational error by a courier plane.

There is an axiom in the intelligence world that the risk of information being leaked increases in proportion to the square of the number of people in the know. Therefore,

The final meeting before the battle was held in an atmosphere of mistrust and maximum security. (*NARA*)

at the beginning, only a few officers working on the project were kept in the know. The circle of insiders was to open up in November 1944. The two main staffs were, of course, kept in the dark because there was still so much to be done in terms of coordination. Jodl emphasised that nothing could be communicated by telephone. At the end of the month, the number of people informed was still increasing, the General der Infanterie Buhle had to be consulted about supplies, the representatives of the Luftwaffe and Kriegsmarine were informed.[15] The Ersatzheer also needed to be involved to speed up formations, and General der Infanterie Gercke, head of OKW transport, also needed to be involved in the organisation.

If instructions and plans were not sent over the air, the same could not be said for the internal traffic of daily operational orders. At this level no restrictions were ordered to the units in line, on the contrary, the OKW wanted everything on the front to appear normal. Of course, the presence of the 5. and 6. Panzer-Armee needed to remain secret and these two large formations were kept in strict radio silence. There was no new command post set up near the front, with the few officers who were invariably present operating under fictitious call signs. This differentiation explains why some instructions directly related to the operation were sent in clear text by the uninitiated. Thus, shortly before the attack, the Luftwaffe was ordered to carry out a reconnaissance of the bridges over the Meuse to ensure that those destroyed during the retreat in September 1944 had been rebuilt. The staff's aim was to select the best possible crossing points on the river. This request did not

At the front, the Americans were preparing for Christmas 1944 in complete ignorance of the storm that was brewing. (*NARA*)

go unnoticed by the Americans. Intercepted by Ultra, it worried General Sibert, the G2 of 12th Army Group. Von Manteuffel explained to his interrogators:

> *There is no doubt that the main factor in the success of the offensive was to surprise the enemy. Because of this, the strictest secrecy had to be maintained, even if it made it more difficult and delayed the concentration of troops. All orders were sealed with security seals. The success proved that the opponent had been completely surprised. The troops were informed that new divisions had recently been organised in the rear, east of the Rhine, and had been assembled for the purpose of relieving the worn-out divisions in the Aachen area.*[16]

When asked specifically about the security measures surrounding the Reich's final surge, Von Manteuffel said that specific instructions were applied in relation to the withdrawal of frontline units in late November and early December 1944. The Germans made an elaborate plan to bring new divisions to the line. As they were temporarily relieved, the units concerned were informed that they were being placed in reserve to meet a future American attack.

This movement was done in three phases. In the first phase, forces from central Germany or Hungary were brought into the Eifel sector. They thus relieved the

False radio activity was maintained on the German side so as not to attract the attention of the enemy. (*Public domain*)

formations in line which could be reinforced and reorganised not far to the rear. Finally, the 6. Panzer-Armee, placed in reserve east of the Rhine, was brought back to the front. In order to camouflage these concentrations as much as possible, the soldiers had their quarters dispersed in many villages behind near where the projected point of departure was, covering their equipment as much as possible. They could not fire or move by day. The general went even further in his assembly area by ordering all motor vehicles to move back 8 kilometres behind the front lines to ensure silence. The formations prepared for the assault were not moved west of the Rhine until shortly before the last meeting with Hitler on 12 December. No reconnaissance was allowed below battalion level, and only the commanders who would guide the first waves were allowed to reconnoitre the terrain. The Stab of the 5. Panzer-Armee was withdrawn from the Aachen sector on 20 November and transferred further south to Mayen. The army changed its name to cover its movements and became a Wehrmacht police unit for the front: the Feldjäger Kommando 3. Its headquarters did not return to Maxweiler in the sector of operations until 15 December.

The same measures were taken for the 6. Panzer-Armee. SS-Brigadenführer Fritz Kraemer says:

> *Security was ensured by keeping the number of people who knew about the attack to a minimum. During the period from 1 to 10 December 1944, only Dietrich, the Ia*[17] *and I knew the plans for the attack. The rest of the Stab, even the Oberquartiermeister,*[18] *thought we were preparing to repel a big US attack. We had a big scare when two gunners from the I. SS-Panzer-Korps were sent to get fire data. We thought they had been captured when they did not return, but later we discovered that one of them was dead and the other had returned to our lines. To misinform the Americans further we set up a new army staff, the 25. Armee, which we positioned in the Gladbach area. It was a completely fake army with insignia, radio call signs and all other means to convince the adversary and the local authorities that we had two armies.*[19]

Theorists Impose their Dreams!

The absolute secrecy surrounding all this preparation was certainly a necessity, but also provided piece of mind for Jodl and his collaborators. They could work in the totally abstract planning that a staff was used to, without having to take into account the implacable reality of the facts. In this way, the work proceeded quickly and the contradictory opinions of field officers could be brushed aside. The non-involvement of

Dietrich (centre, facing Hitler), later emphasised to an aide the lack of resources at his disposal for the offensive. (*NARA*)

junior officers, on the other hand, obliged the OKW to plan everything down to the last detail. But tactics were not their forte, and Von Manteuffel realised this when he learned of the planned orders, which were too theoretical:

> *When I received Hitler's orders, I was astonished to find that they specified even the methods to be used and the timetable for operations. The artillery was to open fire at 07:30 and the infantry was to attack at 11:00. In the meantime, the Luftwaffe was to bomb headquarters and communications. The armoured divisions were not to go into action until after the infantry had broken through. The artillery was spread along the entire length of the attack front. I identified several weaknesses in the planned arrangements and immediately prepared others, which I explained to Model. He agreed, but wryly remarked, "You'd better discuss this with the Führer". I replied, "Alright, if you agree to come with me."*[20]

To make his point and improve the plan, on 3 December the commander of the 5. Panzer-Armee accompanied Model to see Hitler in Berlin. He began by questioning the uncontrollable aspects of the plan: the atmospheric conditions on the day of the attack and the fact that the Luftwaffe might not be able to accomplish its mission in the face of a more powerful Allied air force. He reminded the Führer of the difficulties they had encountered in the Vosges, where it had been impossible to move armoured divisions in

Anti-aircraft searchlights were placed on the front line to create artificial light. (*NARA*)

daylight. He insisted that the only effect achieved by the artillery at 07:30 would be to wake up the Americans, who then had three and a half hours to make their arrangements before the assault. He also pointed out that the German infantry was inferior to that at the beginning of the war and that they would not have the strength to make such a deep penetration, especially in such difficult terrain. The American defences comprised a chain of outposts with a main line of resistance far behind that would be difficult to break through.

After dismantling the tactical instructions that were to be imposed on him, he proposed several modifications. Firstly, the assault should be carried out at 05:30, under cover of darkness, accepting that the artillery could not reach all the objectives, but that its fire could be concentrated on a certain number of sensitive points such as batteries, ammunition depots and headquarters, whose exact location the Germans knew. He also suggested forming shock battalions of the best officers to slip in between the US outposts to take them by surprise. Searchlights provided by the ACD units would illuminate the advance of the 'shock battalions' by projecting their beams onto the clouds, which would reflect them onto the ground. After proposing these modifications to Hitler, he told him that the offensive was only possible if he adopted them. He also insisted that by 16:00 it would be dark, and that if he maintained the original arrangements, the attackers would have only five hours after the start of the attack to achieve success. If his plan was adopted, there would be five and a half hours more for the initial fighting. Then, when night fell, the Panzers would advance by night, breaking through the ranks of the infantry, and at dawn the next day they could then assault the main positions whose approaches had been cleared. At the end of the meeting, the Führer unreservedly adopted the improvements proposed by von Manteuffel.[21]

As can be seen, the practical arrangements proposed were in fact nothing more than tactical common sense, which had been totally absent from the initial project. The problem was that in the northern sector, Dietrich, although informed of the plans on 23 November, did not question anything about his sector. He merely complained that he had not received his equipment when, in truth, he was not aware that it was being transferred…

Von Manteuffel's comments highlight one of the basic problems with the plan: it was theoretical from start to finish, a very fine conceptual construction, but lacking any practical vision. He told Liddell Hart among others that: '*Keitel, Jodl and Warlimont had never been on the line. Their ignorance of the conditions of battle led them to neglect the real difficulties of the war and to encourage Hitler in the belief that his fanciful conceptions were feasible. The Führer readily listened to soldiers who, trained in combat, had practical ideas.*'[22]

In fact, the chimeras were revealed as early as the initial planning stage. At the end of September 1944, when the OKW was informed of the Führer's wishes, it predicted that it would take only six weeks to prepare for the attack. For German thinkers, the squaring of the circle would also lie in the organisation of the railway movements. For security reasons, supplies had to be maintained east of the Rhine. On the other side of the river there were only 'islands' left that allowed rail traffic, as there were many

The German Luftwaffe, under the command of Generalleutnant Adolf Galand (here shaking hands with Hitler), provided an aerial umbrella over Germany to protect the set-up of the offensive. (*NARA*)

interruptions to the lines, for example between Koblenz and Trier. For their organisation, six Panzer-Divisionen needed almost 900 trains to be put into action. On 27 October, von Manteuffel immediately realised that the forecasts were too optimistic:

> *At that moment it was obvious that the operation had to be postponed. I remember exactly that I said on the day of the meeting, realising the state of the railway system in Germany and the time it would take to reorganise personnel and equipment, that the attack could not begin before 10 December, although Generalfeldmarschall Model agreed with my analysis, he insisted that the attack should begin on 1 December.*[23]

Despite Keitel's promises, ammunition was in short supply, especially for the 105mm and 150mm howitzers and for the Nebelwefer. Rationing orders were sent to the other fronts. On 16 December the supplies would be limited to 250 rounds per light howitzer and 150 for the heavy ones.[24]

The strategic camouflage would favour the element of surprise, but keeping the secret would cost a lot in terms of preparation. The commanders, informed too late, did not have enough time to study their mission, reconnoitre the terrain and prepare themselves. As a result, several provisions were neglected. Jodl was fully aware of this, but ignored it. The junior officers, especially in the artillery, took up their positions and studied

Ammunition was stockpiled on the east bank of the Rhine in great secrecy. (*Rights reserved*)

the terrain just before the offensive and had to work with great haste. Artillery usually requires a lot more study when advancing over the ground. Nevertheless, it was felt that the importance of surprise outweighed that of preparation. If the Allies had known about the attack a week before, it would have been certain to fail because they would have positioned several armoured divisions accordingly.

The Panther Ausf G was the main battle tank of the German armoured divisions and had a crew of five. (*Rights reserved*)

Chapter 2

The Storm is Brewing

The Productive Surge

Despite the damage they could cause, the raids by thousands of Allied aircraft did not prevent the Reich's industry from maintaining a high level of production. To be less vulnerable, the industrial fabric was dispersed by the creation of small factories scattered in the countryside, or simply transferred to the east, where the Russians had few strategic bombers. A new order imposed the sixty-hour work week on the available workforce, reinforced by increased severity towards STO workers, while civilian consumption was drastically reduced.

Thanks to all these measures, Albert Speer, the Minister of Armaments and War Production, successfully led the Reich's industry to achieve record yields, producing no less than 2,250,000 tonnes of ammunition, 750,000 rifles, 100,000 machine guns and

The industrial power of the Third Reich was at its peak in 1944, despite the constant Allied bombing. (*Rights reserved*)

Albert Speer, the Führer's architect, was responsible for the success of the armament production plan. (*NAC*)

9,000 artillery pieces during the three months of autumn 1944. Only tank production was reduced, but the shortfall was partly made up by an increase in the number of self-propelled assault guns, such as the Hetzer, which was assembled in factories located in Czechoslovakia, well outside the range of Allied raids. Hitler believed he had a great asset in the form of a new weapon: the Messerschmitt 262, a jet fighter almost twice as fast as any Allied propeller plane. Once these jets could be used in sufficient numbers, the Führer believed the Luftwaffe would finally be able to regain control of the skies over Germany. The same applied to the sea, where new submarines, the Type XXI and Type XXIII, were the only ones with the potential to change the situation by stemming the maritime traffic from across the Atlantic. What the dictator needed more than anything, however, was more time! He knew by now that time for the Third Reich was short: a few months were needed to complete the project. Despite all the crises on the Eastern Front, he could still hope to gain some respite by exchanging time for space. Of course, he was aware that the Russian penetration of East Prussia would have a considerable psychological impact on the German people. However, he also knew there was little in this territory that was absolutely vital for Germany's survival. On the Vistula, the Red

Army was still more than 450 kilometres away from any critical strategic objective, such as the capital Berlin or the mining and industrial areas of Silesia. Moreover, Stalin's summer offensive was running out of steam, with its lines of communication too stretched to support another one before the end of winter. Tactically, he thought he had little to fear from this side, for the time being, at least.

Mastering the Skies

In anticipation of the *Wacht am Rhein* offensive, the Luftwaffe deliberately weakened its defensive power in the Reich's skies and focused a large part of its resources over the area of ground units concentrated between Paderborn and Cologne. To fulfil its mission, the II. Jagd-Korps had 1,492 fighters at its disposal, including the excellent Me Bf 109 K4 and Fw 190 D operating from hard runways. Its first objective was to close the skies to Allied reconnaissance operations. It must be said that it succeeded very well in this, which explains in part Eisenhower's staffs' surprise at the scale of the German operation.[1]

There was one element that greatly disadvantaged the Allied tactical air force, even though it was supposed to be utterly dominant in the European skies in view of its

The latest Messerschmidt 109s line up to take to the skies over the Reich. (*Rights reserved via Erkes*)

plethora of personnel: the incessant rains of the autumn which soaked its airfields. The fields were made of wire mesh laid on beds of straw; despite the ingenuity of their design, many of them were impassable in November and the beginning of the following month. Rainfall severely hampered the accuracy of high-altitude bombing and reconnaissance attempts. Thus, in the preliminary phase of the offensive, the Luftwaffe was able to fulfil its role as an 'air umbrella' perfectly.

Subsequently, the Luftwaffe had to strike a very hard blow against the Allied bases so that, by means of a knockout action, the Allied air forces could be reduced to impotence over the projected battlefield. This operation was named *Bodenplatte* by Hermann Göring. To carry it out, the II. Jagd-Korps had at its disposal the 3. Jagd-Division (JG 1, JG 6, JG 26, JG 54 and JG 7) (JG for Jagdgeschwader, fighter squadron)) whose mission was to attack the British bases located in the north of the sector, while the Jafümittelrhein (JG 2, JG 4 and JG 11) had to attack the American grounds. JG 53, belonging to the 5. Jagd-Division, was responsible for bombing the runways in the Metz area. The group was reinforced by a group of the Kampfgeschwader 51[2] (KG 51) on Me 262s and one of the Schlachtgeschwader[3] 4 (SG 4). Walter Model hoped that after this blow, these means could be used to disrupt the enemies' communications.

The OKW was nevertheless well aware that with its small number of troops, it would not be able to reverse the situation in the skies over Northern Europe. This is why winter was chosen: the bad weather in the region could ground the Allied air force more surely than the Messerschmitts

Generalfeldmarschall Hugo Sperrle issued an order in February 1944 to pacify the rear area of the armies and to eradicate the Maquis, which were forming in ever greater numbers. (*NAC*)

V2 rockets were used to strike the port of Antwerp to disrupt Allied logistics. (*Coll. Micklethwaite*)

The V-weapons were an extremely useful tool as they compensated for the inadequacy of the Luftwaffe's bombing forces. In anticipation of *Wacht am Rhein*, on 12 October 1944, Operation *Donnerschlag* was launched. Two cities were targeted as priorities: London and Antwerp. The first agglomeration was always targeted for psychological reasons, preparing the strategic goal of the ground offensive in the making. The second was targeted for operational reasons: to try to hinder Allied supplies, with fire aimed at the central area of the port city. During the preparatory phase of the Ardennes offensive, from 13 October to 26 November, 556 V2s were launched towards the large Flemish city. A second peak of attacks was reached during the fighting in December, bringing the total to 1,610, without, however, weakening the logistics. It should be noted that Liège, and in particular the American supply centre at Droixhe, was also targeted. The town was hit eighty-six times.[4]

Fuel and Ammunition

The supply of petrol would be the sticking point of the offensive. This SS soldier was lucky enough to be able to fill his tank. (*NARA*)

The real sticking point was synthetic fuel. Raids on German cities did not have much psychological impact because of the police power of the state, but targeted attacks on fuel plants had a catastrophic effect. Destruction operations were carried out by the Allies in a systematic manner. The bombed-out plants were left alone until production was able to resume, when the bombing would then resume in earnest. The method was extremely effective and created a fuel shortage that would play an important role in the great battle that was about to begin. The lack of fuel would be one of the main worries for the commanders going up to the line.

At this level, the German forces had been in a constant state of shortage since April 1944. On 30 June 1944, Albert Speer explained in a report to Hitler that the destruction caused would undoubtedly lead to a shortage of fuel reserves in the autumn. To reduce the military consequences of the situation, petrol was rationed in Germany and farmers had their supplies reduced. Movements were limited to the strict minimum to reserve the precious liquid for combat formations. Speer concluded his message by saying: '*If we do not manage to protect our hydrogenation sites and refineries better, there will be a shortage of fuel supplies that cannot be made up from September of this year.*' In his memoirs, the Minister further explains:

> *At the beginning of December, I was concerned that the training of tank drivers left much to be desired due to insufficient training because of the lack of fuel. General Jodl, of course, knew even better than me what our plight was in this respect. In order to make 17,500 tonnes of fuel available for the Ardennes offensive, which used to take two and a half days to produce, he had to suspend the supply of fuel to other army groups on 10 November 1944. In the meantime, the effect of the bombing on the synthetic hydrocarbon plants had indirectly affected the entire chemical production. I had to inform Hitler "that we had to mix the explosives with salt to fill the existing casings and that we were going to the limit of what was possible". In fact, from October 1944 onwards, the explosives contained 20% rock salt, which reduced their effectiveness accordingly.*[5]

Despite his organisational skills, Speer was never able to match the Allied industrial war machine. (*NAC*)

The shortage of petrol, however, remained the biggest problem facing the German generals. Von Manteuffel told Liddell Hart:

> *Jodl had guaranteed us sufficient petrol supplies to enable us to deploy all our forces and then advance. This did not happen, unfortunately. The OKW established by mathematical and invariable formulas the quantity of petrol necessary to advance a division of 100 kilometres. My experience in Russia had taught me that, on the battlefield, a double quantity was needed. Jodl did not understand this. Considering the extra difficulties to be expected in such rough terrain as the Ardennes in winter, I told Hitler myself that we needed five times the typical ration of petrol. When the battle started, we had only one and a half times the standard amount of petrol. Worse still, it was kept far too far to the rear in long convoys on the east bank of the Rhine. When the fog lifted and the Allied planes could operate, the march of these convoys was severely hampered.*[6]

Staff theorists thought otherwise. The OKW planned 20,000 tonnes of fuel for the operation: 8,000 tonnes to reach the Meuse, another 8,000 for the objectives north of that river and 4,000 in reserve. The army commanders did not know this and their orders to help themselves to captured Allied depots reflected this lack of knowledge. It is true that the OKW thinkers had foreseen that the skies would be overcast, but they could not imagine that Patton would have the impudence to start praying for better weather and be heard by the 'Big Boss'…

Insufficient supplies were distributed at the beginning of the offensive. (*Rights reserved*)

Four days before the offensive, Hitler called a meeting of all corps commanders at his headquarters in Bad Nauheim. Also present were Keitel, Jodl, Von Rundstedt and Model. The Führer wanted this final meeting to explain to his officers the intrinsic reasons for the offensive he had imposed on them. He insisted that the continual withdrawal of the army must stop. All the necessary preparations had been completed and they had a thousand Panzers at their disposal. He dwelled at length on the previous campaigns and emphasised that the German people must no longer be subjected to bombing.

It was in this context of shortages that the units had to build up their reserves for the assault in the Ardennes. In a post-war interview, Fritz Kraemer, the chief of staff of the 6. Panzer-Armee, said:

> *We had enough ammunition for eight days, with another eight days in the depots or on rail convoys en route to the front. I considered that quite adequate. We had enough fuel for an initial advance of 200km. This fuel was not entirely distributed among the divisions, it was partly stored in depots west of the Rhine and partly on the way.*[7]

Kraemer went on to explain that he expected to receive additional supplies from the depots every day. This meant that the reserves of the 6. Panzer-Armee were, in fact, just sufficient to reach Antwerp if all went well. The divisions going up to the front line had only two full tanks, the rest had to be distributed afterwards. In case of problems caused by American air action, orders were given to draw on captured fuel depots. Peiper confirms this:

> *It was later announced that two loads of fuel urgently needed for the offensive had not yet arrived, and consequently orders were given to all units to draw on captured stocks. The divisional intelligence officer had a map to show the American logistic facilities. According to this map, we believed we could capture fuel at Büllingen and Stavelot.*[8]

The Last Conference

Hitler had strong opinions about the planned attack. Jodl explained that his main idea expressed on that day was that the assault should be as broad-based as possible and that the armies should not be launched in an attack on Liège or Aachen, which he considered too important to be taken by surprise.

As he issued his final instructions before the Ardennes offensive, Hitler hoped that his generals would go into battle with the feeling that this was the last chance to change the fate of the Reich. (*NARA*)

The Volks-Grenadiers head to the front line. (*Rights reserved*)

This is why he wanted the Meuse to be crossed west of Liège. He wanted the vanguard units not to worry about their rear, but to push forward across the river in a rapid movement via the undestroyed bridges. That is why they should not stop to capture St. Vith or Bastogne. For him it was now or never, and everything had to be risked because there would be no better opportunity later. He said he had done all he could and was throwing his last reserves into the battle, although they would be needed in the east. However, he maintained that the attack must take place in the west because the Russians had so many troops that even if the German forces were to destroy thirty divisions, it would make no difference. On the other hand, if those thirty divisions were knocked out in the west, it would be a third of the entire Anglo-American force.

At the end of the conference, each officer was given a few minutes to talk to the Führer. When it was Sepp Dietrich's turn, the Führer asked him if his army was ready. The SS general replied: '*Not for an offensive*'. To this the dictator retorted: '*You are never satisfied*'. Dietrich said that the other participants' answer was similar: they were not fully prepared.

A Bad Prospect

The analysis of the testimonies of the German generals reveals an OKW under the orders of the dictator who was increasingly distancing himself from the realities on the ground in his company His decisions were criticised and, to be honest, were indeed open to criticism because they were either utopian or unworkable in practice. The result is what is known in psychology as an emotional detachment from the commanding officer in the field. This state is reflected in a disassociation with the higher levels, a visible loss of involvement both in the manner and in the expected results. In fact, in the autumn of 1944, Hitler was alone in his efforts. Von Rundstedt, Model and their respective staffs did not believe in the success of the operation. Dietrich did not learn about the preparations until almost the day before the attack. Only von Manteuffel stood out from the crowd by his careful preparation of the offensive. Nevertheless, by changing his plans to head for Dinant, he could almost be accused of insubordination. Indeed, he did not believe in the impracticality of the race to Antwerp and organised his position in such a way as to play out his own plan for the second part of the operations.

General der Panzertruppen Hasso Eccard commanded the 5. Panzer-Armee. He did not believe in the success of Hitler's plan, which he considered to be disproportionate to the offensive resources available. (*Rights reserved*)

If the Führer's strategic objective was at least well thought out and based on real prospects for intra-Allied tension, there was still a long way to go. Germany, drained after five years of intensive warfare, no longer had the means to carry out its policy and it was certain that the operation would be lost before it began. This catastrophic aspect of the situation did not escape the German senior officers who, resigned after having tried to change the course of events, implemented a plan to which they gave no chance of success.

The combination of material and numerical inferiority, loss of control over the skies, a utopian plan based on wishful thinking, the detachment of the cadres, and manifest optimism in planning would lead to a predictable catastrophe!

Chapter 3

US Troops Facing the Reich

The 'Weak Link' Under the Microscope

The sector of the Ardennes in which the mass of German armies would strike was only lightly guarded. The Americans preferred to keep their northern and southern wings well stocked in order to be able to go on the offensive at points they considered strategic. As a result, favoured by a sector agreeable to defence, the centre of their position was very extensive.

The sector of the Ardennes in which the mass of German armies would strike was very weakly guarded. On the flanks, two offensives were being prepared. (*NARA*)

With his First US Army, General Courtney Hodges held no less than 200 kilometres of front, from the north of Aachen to the south of the Grand Duchy of Luxembourg. His position was divided into three corps. The VII Corps, commanded by General J. Lawton Collins, with six divisions, attacked on the Roer. It should be noted that this river, which was the last rampart before Cologne, must not be confused with the industrial zone of the Ruhr, which was further north. In this sector, the troops were highly concentrated because until November, they had been facing the 6. Panzer-Armee, which was considered the enemy's strongest and most mobile reserve.

General Leonard T. Gerow's V Corps, with four divisions, aimed for the Seven Lakes area, the key dams of the Roer. Their preliminary capture was necessary before the assault on Cologne because the Germans had to be prevented from flooding the region when the US units were deployed. The junction with VIII Corps in the south of the position was assured by the 99th Infantry Division.

To the south of these two strategic sectors was General Troy Middleton's VIII Corps. It stretched for 120 kilometres with only four divisions: the 106th, 28th, 4th Infantry Divisions; two Combat Commands of the 9th Armored Division and the 14th Cavalry Group. Each division held a front of about 35 kilometres, four times the width generally

General Middleton's VIII Corps sector was particularly stretched. As the battle raged in the Bastogne sector, Middleton is seen here distributing food to an elderly refugee woman. (*NARA*)

The 4th ID occupied the southern flank of VIII Corps. The division was under the command of Major General Raymond O. Barton, who experienced the anguish of the German attack from the very first hours of the offensive. (*NARA*)

accepted for a unit of this echelon. Their support points were so far apart that they could not cross their fire.

Middleton was rightly concerned about the operational value of his corps. General Jones' 106th Infantry Division, in line east of St. Vith, was made up of 'rookies' who had come straight from the United States. Although the 28th Infantry Division was more seasoned, it had to train the 6,000 or so replacements who had taken the place of those killed, wounded and missing in the violent clashes in the Hürtgen Forest. The 14th Cavalry Group was in relatively good shape, having already had combat experience during the siege of Brest. Its units spread from Lützkampen to Wallendorf. The 4th Infantry Division was a formation of veterans resting from their hard engagements around Aachen. Some of its battalions had only 40% of their organic strength. The 9th Armored Division had never seen action and had been in its sector for just six days. Recently landed from the USA, it was immediately deprived of two Combat Commands, one assigned to V Corps and another taken to serve as a tactical reserve within Middleton's own grouping.

Middleton's requests for reinforcements were denied as his sector was considered passive, and the higher echelons, the First US Army (FUSA) and the 12th Army Group, had no other fresh troops. At his level, Middleton had only Combat Command R (Colonel Joseph H. Gilbreth) of the 9th Armored Division as a tactical reserve. If necessary, he could use the four engineer battalions of VIII Corps and the three engineer battalions received in support from the FUSA as infantry.

Compared to the German strength, it appears that each major American unit would be engaged by forces four times as large. By way of comparison, for the OKW this was as good a balance of power as General Ludendorff had on 21 March 1918 during his last spring offensive.

To the south of this very stretched device, facing the Saar against which he was preparing an offensive, was Patton. The Third Army of the ebullient general had a considerable strike force: the 4th and 6th Armored Divisions, the 5th, 26th, 35th, 80th, 85th, 90th and 95th Infantry Divisions and two Cavalry Groups. In the event of an attack on the Ardennes salient, some of these units could be directed north, while the remainder could be placed in a defensive position without too much difficulty. Fearing an attack to the north of his sector, Patton also had plans prepared in advance for the pivoting of part of his troops, in order to be prepared for any eventuality…

In the north, the Ninth Army also has large reserves to throw into the battle.

The Challenges of Victory

Hitler was right to target the logistics hub of Antwerp. Access to the port had only just been opened and the Allies could finally breathe a sigh of relief. It is important to realise that the Allies' victory in the European theatre in 1944-1945 could not have been achieved without an efficient supply chain. When the United States entered the war,

Storms in the English Channel had temporarily disrupted Allied logistics at the start of Operation *Overlord* by destroying the American artificial harbour. (*NARA*)

Despite undeniable logistical organisation, the speed of the Allied armies' advance was hampered by a lack of supplies. (*NARA*)

few regular army officers had any training or experience in transport. The skills were to be found in the railways, shipping and road transport companies, many of whom were enlisted in the US Army. These neophyte officers were to become familiar with army methods and to set up efficient procedures for transferring men and material from armament factories to ports of embarkation. From December 1943 until the end of the war in Europe, the number of passengers embarking for overseas destinations exceeded 200,000 per month. The record was set in January 1945, with 295,000 soldiers sent. Usually about 66% of the passengers were sent to Atlantic destinations and the other third to the Pacific.[1]

After the invasion of Normandy, despite the lack of deep-water ports and the destruction of the American artificial harbours of Utah and Omaha beaches by a storm, the landing of supplies would not decrease.[2]

The progression of troops and the arrival of additional divisions in France obliged the Allies to set up a supply system commensurate with the successes achieved on the ground. The first difficulty encountered was to restore the various communication routes to working order. The tactical and strategic aviation of the Allies, as well as the action of the Resistance, put out of use the great majority of the communication routes in order to prevent and delay the arrival of the German reinforcements. Uncle Sam's pioneers worked miracles to restore the transport network to an optimal level within a very short time.

Via the Expressways

As soon as Paris was liberated, a lack of road transport meant that supplies piled up in the ports and on the beaches. The front was no longer adequately supplied. As they flew from victory to victory, the Allied armies were on the verge of running out of fuel. Faced with this crisis, the US Army gathered all available trucks and pooled them to create transport units from depots to theatres of operation. The principle was based on a one-

The Red Ball Express journey began on the beaches of France. (*NARA*)

GMCs consumed a lot of fuel to bring supplies to the front line. The further the front line moved away from the logistics bases, the more complicated the situation became. (*NARA*)

way loop route. This is how the most famous of these distribution systems was born: the Red Ball Express.

In service from 25 August to 16 November 1944, it lasted only three months, but in those 81 days, 23,000 men using 6,000 trucks and trailers carried more than 412,193 tonnes of supplies to the American armies on the march from Normandy to the German border.[3] The cessation of the Red Ball Express coincided with the closure of the ports at Utah and Omaha beaches and the opening of the port of Antwerp.

Another 'express' route was set up to provide equipment, mainly fuel, for the 21st Army Group's Operation *Market Garden:* the Red Lion Express. The latter was launched on 16 September and ended on 12 October, after twenty-seven days of operation. It was made up of eight American transport companies, six of which were equipped with 2.5-ton GMCs and two with 10-ton semi-trailers. These vehicles were taken from the Red Ball Express and made the long journey from Caen to Bayeux to Brussels, an approximate 1,000km loop.[4] This new route benefitted from the experience acquired with the Red Ball Express, with improvements being made and the average daily tonnage increasing to 650 tonnes per day instead of the planned 500.

On 6 October, another expressway was opened: the White Ball Route. This route was organised on shorter routes than the first two and carried supplies from the newly opened ports of Le Havre and Rouen. Its mission was to transport supplies either directly

The port of Cherbourg was heavily sabotaged by the Germans and divers were used to reopen the port to traffic. (*NARA*)

to the armies or in transit to the rail network in Paris or Reims. The road was closed on 10 January 1945.

On 18 December 1944, two days after the beginning of the Ardennes offensive, 274 2.5-ton trucks of the White Ball Route and 258 others of the Seine section were requisitioned to transport the 82nd and 101st Airborne to the Ardennes front.[5] The next day, the White Ball Route released 347 additional trucks for the redeployment of Patton's Third Army.

The opening of the port of Antwerp changed the situation; the ports on the landing beaches were closed and the Red Ball Express route was closed. On 28 December 1944, the port facilities received 111,347 tonnes of supplies, compared with 37,091 in Cherbourg, 50,491 in Le Havre and 41,311 in Rouen.[6] A new route was born: ABC Haul.[7] Although the port of Antwerp was in the zone of influence of the British and the Canadians, the Allies shared the port installations, and the ABC Haul remained strictly American. Its mission: to relieve the congestion of the port of Antwerp and to supply the large depots located in Mons, Charleroi and Liège.

All Roads lead to the Front

After the liberation of Paris on 27 August, it became clear that road transport was reaching its limits. A formidable task of rebuilding the network by the Americans and public service personnel was undertaken in order to allow the transport of large tonnage and delivery directly to the advanced bases from the ports that had to be decongested. In December, the daily average levels of supplies leaving the ports was as follows:

- By rail 19,079 tonnes
- By truck 3,771 tonnes
- By pipeline 3,503 tonnes
- By waterways 657 tonnes
- By air 398 tonnes[8]

Pipelines were quickly implemented to supply the armies near the front line. (*NARA*)

At the end of September 1944, SHAEF planners estimated the daily requirement per division to be 560 tonnes in an army group,[9] to be distributed as follows:[10]

Class I: 78 tonnes, 14%
Class II: 75 tonnes, 13%
Class III: 144 tonnes, 26%
Class IV: 110 tonnes, 20%
Class V: 153 tonnes, 27%

Class I: Food and drink.
Class II: Individual clothing, tents, small tools, maps, administrative, and household supplies and equipment.
Class III: Fuels, lubricants, hydraulic oils, bulk chemicals, refrigerants, de-icers and anti-freeze, petroleum and chemical additives and coal.
Class IV: Construction and fortification materials.
Class V: Ammunition of all types, bombs, explosives, mines, detonators and pyrotechnics.
Class VI: Personal demand items (such as health and hygiene products, soaps and toothpaste, writing materials, snacks, drinks, cigarettes, batteries, alcohol, cameras and non-military sales items).
Class VII: Heavy equipment, mobile workshops, tanks and vehicles.
Class VIII: All medical equipment except consumables.
Class VIII Medical equipment, including repair parts specific to medical equipment.
Class VIIIa Included consumable medical supplies, excluding blood and blood products.
Class VIIIb Included blood and blood components (whole blood, platelets, plasma, packed red blood cells, etc.).
Class IX: Tools required for the maintenance or repair of equipment.
Class X: Equipment to support non-military programmes such as agriculture and economic development (not included in classes I-IX). Salvage and captured equipment.

Symbols Used

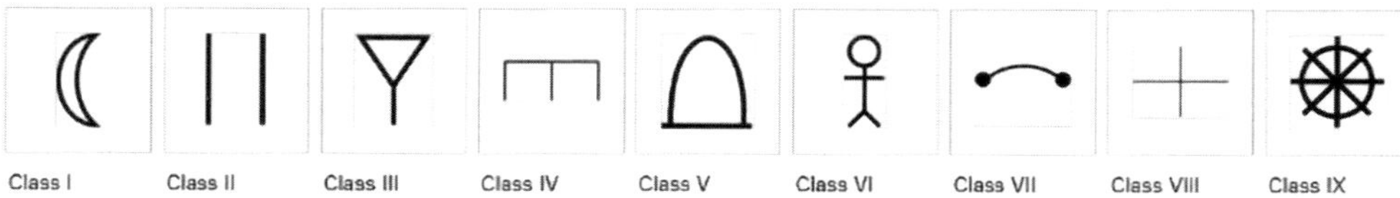

The Liège Logistics Hub

Air supply, although representing very small quantities compared to the overall figures, was particularly used for POL (petrol oil and lubricants), which was considered the most urgent. During the Battle of the Bulge, the base at Bierset, close to the front, became an important supply centre for fuel. An airlift between the base and Great Britain was started. The airfield received several hundred Dakota C47s, which were filled with precious fuel every day. At certain times of the day a C47 landed every 20 or 30 seconds. When the field was full, the Dakotas waited in groups of twenty-four for permission to land. Landing docks were provided for unloading 200-litre drums, which were rolled directly into trucks that headed for Beyne-Heusay (Belgium). There, the petrol was decanted into 20-litre jerry cans to be transported to the front line. Once unloaded, the C47s took on board the seriously wounded, accompanied by nurses, to await treatment in England.[11]

The Allies did not attach any importance to the waterways, claiming that the rehabilitation work was too costly in relation to the services provided. The exception

Due to the seriousness of the situation, emergency supplies were delivered by air. (*NARA*)

was the Albert Canal, linking Antwerp to the river port of Liège. It was a route of direct military value to Hodges' First US Army and Simpson's Ninth Army. The British made the Antwerp canal operational as far as Maasmechelen, while the Americans took care of the rest as far as Monsin Island in Liège, which served as a rear logistics base for the port of Antwerp.[12] Liège, supplied by the ports of Antwerp and Ostend, became the main forward depot for the First US and Ninth armies.[13]

Adapting the Rules

The tonnage allocation system operated on a flat-rate system based on average consumption. If successful, the procedure inevitably resulted in the accumulation of a flow of items not deemed essential. In order to continue the advance, the stocks in the armies gradually become unbalanced. In addition, the period from 8 November to 16 December was marked by a continuous improvement in supplies thanks to the opening of Antwerp and the improvement of the rail network. Changes in the supply procedure were required and tonnage allocations to the armies were abolished. A ten-day requisition procedure for all supplies, except ammunition, was introduced.[14]

The improved performance of fuel logistics allowed armies to set up large reserves close to the front in preparation for imminent offensive operations aimed at the heart of Germany. By 16 December 1944, in Bradley's 12th Army Group, Hodges' First US Army had seven days' supply of directly available fuel. Meanwhile, Patton's Third Army had 8.8 days, while Simpson's Ninth Army had 12.8 days.[15]

The Albert Canal was used extensively to transport supplies from Antwerp to Liège. (*Rights reserved*)

By the end of summer 1944, the logistical situation on the Continent was gradually stabilising. (*NARA*)

At the beginning of December 1944, the First US Army has its HQ in the famous spa town of Spa, the POL strategic was composed of two main depots, which were installed in the immediate vicinity. The first one above Spa, the other near Stavelot. The reserve amounted to 12,300 tonnes (14,820,000 litres or 3,915,000 US gallons)[16] divided as follows: 80% petrol with 80 octane, the remaining 20% consisting of lubricants, antifreeze, coolant, brake oils, etc. A real Ali Baba's barracks easily accessible to the Panzer-Division, which had to bypass Liège by the south and was in desperate need of supplies.

The first depot was located at 'Le Rosier', at the intersection of the La Gleize–Spa roads towards Andrimont. It extended from the crossroads to the Bérinzenne estate and had 2,226,000 US gallons (8,426,000 litres) of petrol and related products.

The second depot at Haute Levée in Stavelot had 1,115,000 US gallons (4,220,000 litres) of petrol and related products and was located on the old Stavelot–Francorchamps road. It was guarded by Belgian fusiliers of the 5th Fusiliers Battalion, originally from Charleroi. The third depot was on the road to the Francorchamps circuit,[17] shortly after the road to Cheneux. The fourth depot was on the old Stavelot–Malmedy road at the hamlet of Bista. These latter two stockpiles contained the remainder of the POL, i.e. 574,000 US gallons.

From all these arrangements, it is clear that the area under attack by the 6. Panzer-Armee was full of fuel. This would become an element of uncertainty in the battle ahead. If the Germans captured the US supplies, they would solve one of their initial problems; their lack of preparation.

Chapter 4

KG Peiper Prepares

The 6. Panzer-Armee's Setup

The sector of Stavelot–La Gleize, our main focus here, was overseen by the 6. Panzer-Armee. Its leader, SS-Oberstgruppenführer Sepp Dietrich, described its creation in view of the Battle of the Bulge:

> *The army was formed between September and October '44 in Westphalia with the 1., 2., 9. and 12. SS-Panzer-Divisionen. Later the 12. Volks-Grenadier-Division (VGD) and 3. Fallschirmjäger-Division (FJD) and other infantry units were added. At the time of the Ardennes, the 6. Armee was not an SS army, but a regular army. The headquarters in Berlin would not allow it to become SS until April 1945, when we were in Hungary, because I had SS and Wehrmacht troops under my command. In Hungary there was another sixth army*[1] *and to distinguish the two my army was designated 6. SS-Panzer-Armee. At that time, I had only SS troops with me.*[2]

For his assault, Sepp Dietrich had:

- I. SS-Panzer-Korps, consisting of the 1. and 12. SS-Panzer-Divisionen, Otto Skorzeny's Panzer-Brigade 150, the 277. and 12. Volks-Grenadier-Divisionen and the 3. Fallschirmjäger-Division
- SS-schwere Panzer-Abteilung 501 with 45 Tiger II
- II. SS-Panzer-Korps, covering the 9. and 2. SS-Panzer-Divisionen
- LXVII. Korps, comprising the 246., 272. and 326. Volks-Grenadier-Divisionen
- schwere Panzer-Abteilung 506 with 38 Tiger II and 9 Tiger I
- schwere Panzerjäger-Abteilung 653 with Jagdtiger
- Sturmpanzer-Abteilung 217 equipped with Sturmpanzer IV[3]
- and finally, various corps artillery units including three Volks-Artillerie-Korps, two Volks-Werfer-Brigaden and three heavy artillery Abteilungen[4]

While this armoured army appears powerful, in reality, Dietrich stated that its level of training was average, with 60% of the combat elements having less than six to eight weeks of exercise. A Panzer-Division had 17-18,000 men, of which 9-10,000 were used in service tasks. The majority of the reinforcements came from the Luftwaffe, the Kriegsmarine and other army units. Most of them were young men between the ages of 18 and 25. The manoeuvres were carried out up to battalion level and no higher and they

A vigil by an armoured unit at the front. (*Rights reserved*)

received only basic training. The main problem was a lack of fuel.[5] In total, its strength was about 500 tanks, but during the approach march, some 20% would break down.

This mechanical attrition rate was huge in the eyes of the Allies, but considered normal by Dietrich, as the mechanical reliability of the Panther and Tiger II left something to be desired.

Apart from a first working meeting mentioning the hypothetical launch of an operation on 23 November, the SS-Obergruppenführer claimed that he had only been warned of the offensive on 12 December during a meeting in which Hitler had invited his main commanders. The 6. Panzer-Armee then had only four days to prepare. Dietrich felt that this was not enough and dared to tell the Führer, insisting, in particular, on his lack of fuel. He was told that he would have everything he needed…[6] Leaving the briefing, the general received his detailed orders, which had been prepared in advance by Model's staff. The 6. Panzer-Armee had only two days to disseminate the instructions to the lower echelons. Time was short, and the assault was delayed by one day. The Battle of the Bulge finally began on 16 December 1944.

The Volks-Grenadiers brought together men of all arms and were supervised by veterans of the Eastern Front. These men, who were generally good quality basic recruits, were sent to the front under the direction of experienced officers. (*Rights reserved*)

It was the I. SS-Panzer-Korps who led the way, with the 12. SS-Panzer-Division on the right in the Krinkelt-Rocherath-Wirttzfeld area, the 1. SS-Panzer-Division 'Leibstandarte SS Adolf Hitler' in the centre via the Losheim Gap,

Two Tiger II battalions participated in the offensive. This example dates from 1944 and is still covered in Zimmerit anti-magnetic paste. It is a command tank, recognisable by its star antenna. (*NARA*)

The Panzer IV theoretically equipped the second battalion of a Panzer Regiment in 1944. (*Rights reserved*)

Jodl told Dietrich that his reconnaissance elements had to arrive on the Meuse on the first day. He is photographed here with his second wife, Ursula Moninger-Brenner. (*NARA*)

Büllingen, Stavelot, La Gleize and the 12. Volks-Grenadier-Division on the left, in the area of Holzheim, Honsfeld, Heppenbach and Medendorf.

The II. SS-Panzer-Korps was initially held in reserve in the event of a counter-attack by the Ninth US Army from the north. If this happened, it would have to protect the northern flank and repel the attempt. This option was guaranteed until the I. SS-Panzer-Korps reached the Meuse. Finally, if the initial assault failed, the II. SS-Panzer-Korps would have to advance to the St. Vith–Vielsalm line. In the meantime, the units needed to remain ready to leave their assembly areas located 30 to 40 kilometres behind the front. In fact, the 2. SS-Panzer-Division would set off on 22 December and follow a route further south, parallel to that of the 1. SS-Panzer-Division 'Leibstandarte SS Adolf Hitler'. It could not do so earlier because of a fuel shortage.

Jodl told Dietrich that his reconnaissance elements were to arrive at the Meuse on the first day, followed by the bulk of them on the second or third day! This statement made the SS-Obergruppenführer jump, to the point that he reproached the chief of staff for remaining at the level of the Kriegsspiel without considering the reality of the terrain. It should be noted that although Skorzeny's Panzer-Brigade 150 was officially an integral part of the 6. Panzer-Armee, its action remained completely independent. The special unit's aim was to create confusion in the opponent's rear and, if possible, seize bridges by surprise.

The Troublesome Flank

The 6. Panzer-Armee remained in reserve in the Cologne area after its creation to allow the divisions belonging to the I. and II. SS-Panzer-Korps to reconstitute themselves, while at the same time being given the task of reacting to an airborne attack. Contrary to Dietrich's assertion, on 16 November 1944, the most senior members of his staff were

This Panther Ausf G left the factory in the late autumn of 1944 and went straight into the unit. (*Rights reserved*)

informed of the plan for an offensive in the west. Of the two options on the table, Hitler chose the one aimed at Antwerp. The first written instructions concerning the attack arrived on 20 November. They were to be kept strictly secret and known only to the army commander, SS-Oberstgruppenführer and Panzer Generaloberst der Waffen-SS Sepp Dietrich and his chiefs of staff. Their mission was as follows:

> *With the infantry divisions assigned to it, the 6. Panzer-Armee must break through the enemy's defensive front in the Monschau–Krewinkel sector after a strong artillery preparation, then assault with the armoured groups in the direction of the south of Liège without taking care of its rear flanks*[7] *and cross the Meuse river ... secure its right flank on the Albert canal and advance without stopping towards Antwerp.*

Dietrich launches his troops into the attack. (*NARA*)

The order given was therefore very precise regarding the need to advance quickly, and it relied on the disorganisation of the Americans' reaction to succeed in the first phase of the breakthrough. It was the speed and initial shock that would protect the army's flanks in depth. According to the initial plans, the LXVII. Armee-Korps was to hold the right shoulder of the offensive on the general Monschau–Verviers–Liège line. Its main mission was to cut the Eupen–Monschau and Eupen–Malmedy roads, and to relieve Von Der Heydte's Fallschirmjäger, who were supposed to block the La Belle Croix crossroads to prevent any American reinforcements moving towards the attacked sector.[8] It would then return to the 15. Armee, which also had to go on the offensive to fix the American troops in the sector north of Sepp Dietrich's units as soon as the Meuse was crossed. The idea of joining the Albert Canal allowed two things to happen: on the one hand, to encircle Liège and its logistical depots and, on the other, to take advantage of the protection offered by the Albert Canal, a wet cut dug by Belgium during the inter-war period.

At the Planspiel held in the Brühl area south of Cologne, in which the Panzer-Divisionen commanders took part, two major problems were identified.

Firstly, the poor quality of the available infantry units was underlined. If the good performance at the front of the 12. Volks-Grenadier-Division (VGD) was recognised, that of the 3. Fallschirmjäger-Division seems to have left something to be desired. The main fear was that its night attack to break through the defensive front would fail. As its fighters were not sufficiently trained in night infantry combat, the SS leadership

The main challenge for the 6. Panzer-Armee was to cross the Meuse on the third day of the offensive. (*NARA*)

feared they would get lost. As a result, it was the Panzer units that had to do the work, and they were confronted with an American front that had already been alerted by the first unsuccessful attack. To avoid this pitfall, it was planned that 200 anti-aircraft searchlights belonging to the II. Flak-Korpswould be used to illuminate the terrain.

Secondly, the area planned for the initial assault was not at all practical for the use of armoured units. There were only five possible routes to the west. The four southern ones would be devoted to the advance of the armoured units, while the northern one was reserved for the infantry to secure the northern wing of the attack. If the attack failed, the armoured flank of the 6. Panzer-Armee would be completely uncovered. It was therefore planned to ensure success in this sector by the temporary allocation of an

The good performance of the 12. Volks-Grenadier-Division at the front was recognised after the battle. As can be seen here, its personnel were relatively young. (*Rights reserved*)

armoured task force to help open the road for the infantry before returning to its mission on its own route. As the entire armoured task force was intended to drive towards the Meuse, this deviation could in no way diminish the offensive capability of the armoured units.[9]

V Corps was also about to go on the offensive in this sector and massed seasoned infantry units in front of Monschau. (*NARA*)

Thus, as soon as more pragmatic and wiser minds looked at the battle plan envisioned by the OKW theorists, it seemed absurd not to take into account the security of the northern flank. The threat seemed all the greater as the V Corps was preparing to go on the offensive in this sector and was massing seasoned infantry units in front of Monschau. A threat that the 15. Armee could hardly counteract with sufficient reinforcements. Therefore, an armoured reserve was formed to face a possible American victory in this sector, a reserve kept fresh which, in case of success of the first wave of assault, would in time come to take over the forward movement.

Orders and Strike Force of I. SS-Panzer-Korps

In the end, the battle plan of the 6. Panzer-Armee was in accordance with the instructions of the OKW, but the lack of roads and the need for an armoured reserve forced it to spread its resources in two waves. In the first wave, the I. SS-Panzer-Korps (SS-Pz-Kp) of SS-Gruppenführer Hermann Priess would attack at the front with two SS-Panzer-Divisionen (SS-Pz-Div) side by side, the 12. SS-Pz-Div 'Hitlerjugend' of SS-Standartenführer Hugo Kraas on the right wing (north) and the 1. SS-Pz-Div 'Leibstandarte SS Adolf Hitler' of SS-Oberführer Wilhelm Mohnke on the left wing (south). SS-Gruppenführer Wilhelm Bittrich's II. SS-Pz-Kp stood ready to intervene in the second wave with its two large, armoured formations, the 2. SS-Pz-Div 'Das Reich' and the 9. SS-Pz-Div 'Hohenstaufen'.

The initial breakthrough needed to be achieved by three infantry divisions. From north to south there was the 277. VGD in front of Elsenborn, the 12. VGD stretching from Nidrum to Weywertz and the 3. FJD south from Schoppen to Elbergdingen. The

The morale of the German soldiers was very high when the offensive was announced. (*Public domain*)

The Tiger II battalion was in the second line to exploit the breakthrough. (*Public domain*)

whole was to be supported by a Heeres-Sturmgeschutz-Abteilung. It was planned that after the initial breakthrough, these three divisions would return to the upper echelon to attack further north. In the sector of the 1. SS-Pz-Div, which is of particular interest here, the breakthrough was to be made in two distinct phases. The 3. FJD was to open a gap through which the reconnaissance and infantry elements of the 1. SS-Pz-Div (KG Knittel) would first infiltrate along the Krewinkel–Manderfeld–Medendorf–Valender–Born–Recht axis. This advance was supposed to protect the southern flank of KG Peiper, including the reinforced SS-Panzer-Regiment 1, which was to follow the Lanzerath–Honsfeld–Ligneuville–Stavelot axis.[10]

SS-Gruppenführer Priess had a powerful strike force at his disposal for the attack, but it was not as complete as he would have liked. The rehabilitation of the divisions, which had been severely tested by the first phase of the campaign in the west, was far from complete.

Corps Units

A corps has two categories of units: the divisions which are supposed to be able to operate on their own and are in charge of fighting the main battle, and the units which depend directly on the corps and whose mission is to support or sustain the former.

To carry out such an attack, Priess had to be able to count on powerful artillery. He therefore had several artillery regiments at his disposal. First of all, there was the Heeres-Artillerie-Korps 6, which was the size of a division with three regiments. This formation oversaw all the artillery of the 6. Panzer-Armee, including the three Artillerie-Körper of its two Panzer-Korps (the Artillerie Körper (Arko) 101 and 102) and the LXVII AK (the Arko 3696).[11] This was logical insofar as Priess was in charge of the whole initial attack of Dietrich's army. In addition, there were two Volks-Artillerie-Korps and two Volks-Werfer-Brigaden. The availability of ammunition was very limited. There was only one full supply to support the offensive and half a supply to be fired during the artillery preparation fire.

The Divisions Headed by I. SS-Panzer-Korps

The three infantry divisions mentioned above were not assigned to Priess' armoured corps until 14 December, only two days before the offensive began. This is obviously a very short time to settle the countless details inherent in such an operation. The commanders did not know each other, or if they did, only very briefly. Generalmajor Engel, in charge of the 12. VGD, only knew Priess by sight, while the other two, Oberst Viebig in charge of the 277. VGD and Generalmajor Wadehn commanding the 3. FJD, were completely unknown to him. The two VGDs had their ranks filled to about 80%, while the 3.FJD had only three quarters of its organic personnel. It must be remembered, however, that since 24 November, it had been engaged in hard defensive fighting west of Düren under the command of Generalmajor Wadehn. It was only on 13 December that it was detached from this defensive front and did not start its march to its assembly place in St. Vith until the 15th, from where it was to attack on the 16th. As Generalmajor Schimpf, commander of this division, had not yet recovered from his wounds received in Normandy, Generalmajor Wadehn commanded the division.[12]

The two armoured divisions were a little better off, with at least 90% of their personnel. The armoured personnel of the 1. SS-Pz-Div amounted to forty-two Panthers, including four commanders, thirty-seven Panzer IVs, five StuG IIIs, twenty-one Jagdpanzer IVs and eight Flakpanzer IVs, in addition to the Tiger IIs of the SS-Pz-Abt 501. The machines of the 12. SS-Pz-Div included forty-one Panthers, including four commanders, thirty-seven Panzer IVs, twenty-two Jagdpanzers IVs and eight Flakpanzers IVs, plus the PanzerJäger-Abteilung with twenty-eight additional Jagdpanzers IVs and twelve Jagdpanthers. Its personnel was more complete and numbered 23,500 men.

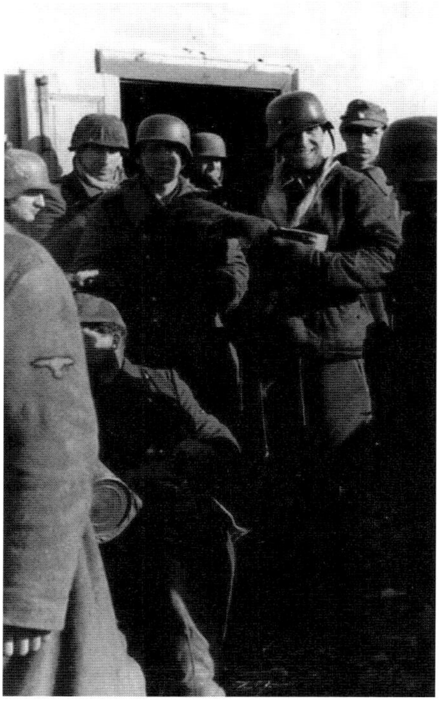

The three conventional infantry divisions were not assigned to Priess' armoured corps until 14 December. (*Rights reserved*)

KG Hansen had the StuG Abteilung of the 1. SS-Panzer-Division. (*NARA*)

The Jagdpanzer IV l/70 was the anti-tank element of KG Hansen. (*NARA*)

KG Knittel comprised the reconnaissance tanks, which were brought to the front by rail. (*Coll. Private*)

A general weakness of all the units of the I. SS-Panzer-Korps was the provision of liaison vehicles, which were at barely 80%. This particularly included light vehicles and heavy semi-trailers, for which Priess spoke of a real shortage, to the point where many artillery pieces had to be towed by trucks, which reduced their mobility.

Finally, there was the problem of distributing the fuel to the units. It was planned that five full tanks would be distributed, two in the tanks and jerry cans carried on board and three in the logistics train. It is clear that this was far from being the case. On the morning of 15 December, the 1. SS-Pz-Div had only 40% of a full tank and the 12. SS-Pz-Div had 60%. It took the intervention of Generalfeldmarschall Model, who was in the Panzer-Korps combat command post on the eve of the assault, for an additional tank to be brought up in extremis. In total, the two armoured divisions had 1.2 and 1.3 full tanks at their disposal, a quantity of petrol that barely allowed them to cover between 60 and 70 kilometres.[13] They were therefore practically threatened with bankruptcy before even starting their attacks.

The tip of the German offensive, which in theory should be the best off because of its importance to the course of the operation, was therefore far from being in perfect operational condition.

Four Kampfgruppen in the Attack

Since the advent of the trenches in 1914, breaking through the enemy's front line has been the major problem in developing an offensive. Tanks were initially invented to facilitate penetration of the enemy's position, but three corollary problems soon rapidly appeared.

The first was the need to exploit the initial breakthrough in the depth of the opponent's lines. This exploitation is essential to destroy the lines of communication and to initiate large encirclements of the enemy troops, which the Germans call a Kessel (cauldron). The infantry units following the armour would be responsible for annihilating them. In addition, the breaking of communication lines made all enemy formations on the front impotent, and, for lack of orders, they thus remained inactive and eventually disintegrated. To achieve this, the Germans were the first to develop a concept of an effective armoured division capable of combining the trio of tanks, infantry and artillery at its level. To improve tactical efficiency, the concept of a Kampfgruppe, or 'battlegroup' was invented. The principle was to conduct the battle by distributing specific missions to the main officers, with a specific combat group being formed to carry out the mission. The advantage was that the necessary resources were concentrated under one head, which favoured coordination in the heat of battle. The concept is still used today, notably in the French army under the name of the *Groupement tactique interarmes*. It should be noted that the German vision of joint combat does not imply a transfer of competence from one arm to another. Infantrymen and armoured vehicles fought together, but fulfilled their roles independently. The coordination of the elements was only at the level of the objective to be achieved. It was the flexible combination of means rather than rigid cooperation that made success possible.

In accordance with this tactical doctrine, the 1. SS-Panzer-Division 'Leibstandarte SS Adolf Hitler' was divided into several combat groups (Kampfgruppen), to carry out its mission.

Kampfgruppe Peiper

Kampfgruppe[14] Peiper was at the tip of this device, in the *Spitze* (point), as the German strategists say. The means placed at Peiper's disposal would operate by seeking to force

Peiper's armoured column on the eve of the assault. Snow had already fallen in the Eifel. (*Rights reserved*)

An Sd.Kfz. 251/9 Ausf D supporting the Schnelle Gruppe Knittel. (*Coll. Private*)

the American defences so as to open up the route to the Meuse, and then, beyond that, to Antwerp.

Its armoured force included two companies of Panther Ausf Gs and two of Panzer IV Ausf Hs from Abteilungen I and II of the 1. SS-Panzer-Regiment. This is why the unit included the Panzer-Kompanien 1, 2, 6 and 7. In this case, these tanks were surrounded by the Stab of the I Abteilung of SS-Sturmbannführer Werner Poetschke.

A Panzer-Regiment normally consisted of four Panther Kompagnien and four Panzer IVs. The losses of autumn 1944 did not allow the organisation chart of the 1. SS-Pz-Div to get back up to their theoretical numbers. So, as a replacement, Peiper was given forty-five brand new Tiger IIs belonging to Heinz von Westernhagen's schwere SS-Panzer-Abteilung 501. Such heavy tank formations were supposed to work independently for one-off actions at the front when the need arose. It is a fact that these machines were very impressive. However, their 69 tonnes and long 8.8cm KwK 43 L/71 gun would make them very difficult to manoeuvre and deploy on the narrow Ardennes roads, where their gargantuan fuel consumption would also prove to be an incapacitating logistical burden.

To light the Panzers' march and escort them, the Panzergrenadiere and half-tracks of SS-Sturmbannführer Josef 'Jupp' Diefenthal's III. (Gep)/SS-Panzer-Grenadier-Regiment 2 were placed at the disposal of Joachim Peiper. These armoured infantrymen were mounted on Schutzepanzerwagen, armoured half-tracks specially designed to carry the infantrymen fighting alongside the Panzer. These were Sd.Kfz. 251 Ausf D. As these vehicles were very versatile, there were many different versions adapted to the different roles their occupants had to fulfil: from simple transport to anti-tank, artillery or anti-aircraft support. There were also specific versions for pioneer units.

SS-Sturmbannführer Werner Poetschke commanded the Peiper Panther. (*Rights reserved*)

During the great offensives of 1918, the victorious armies returned to speed of movement. It very quickly became apparent that the artillery had to be able to follow the movement in order to be able to continue to support the progression of the leading elements. It had to become as mobile as the tank/fantasin pair. The semi-tracked tractors quickly showed their weaknesses at the beginning of the conflict, so the idea of mounting tracked artillery appeared. The self-propelled artillery was born from this need to provide support in depth. Peiper received armoured artillery to facilitate his breakthrough, which included 150-mm guns, self-propelled Sd.Kfz. 138/1s of the 13. (IG)/SS-Panzer-Grenadier-Regiment

The sappers of III. (Gep)/SS-Panzer-Pionier-Battalion 1 accompanied Kampfgruppe. They mainly carried out mine clearance and assault crossing missions. (*Rights reserved*)

2, parachutists of the Fallschirmjäger-Regiment 9 under the command of Oberst von Hoffmann. In this instance, IG stands for Infanterie-Geschutz (infantry gun).

Since the Allies had control of the skies, the German commanders' main fear came from the Jagdbomber, the fighter-bombers of the Allied tactical air force. To protect themselves, the Flak-Sturm-Abteilung 84 (Sf.) of Major von Sacken and the Flakpanzer IV Wirbelwinds of the 10. (Flak)/SS-Panzer-Regiment 1 had the task of building an anti-aircraft umbrella.

The sappers of the III. (Gep)/SS-Panzer-Pionier-Battalion 1 accompanied the Kampfgruppe and mainly carried out mine clearance and assault crossing missions.

KG Peiper was a formation designed to be self-sufficient, comprehensive and to operate using the resources of a joint battle. Its ranks included elite personnel, a very solid mix of veterans and young recruits who believed in the final victory. The mission of the battle group was to reach the River Meuse in the Huy area in two days, cross it and then head for Antwerp. It had to rush forward without worrying about its flanks. It would be up to the task, or so it believed, but the devil was in the details. Not enough fuel had been delivered, and the Kampfgruppe had only received the equivalent of two of the five tanks it had been promised. If it did not receive refuelling en route, it risked running out completely. The mix of medium and heavy equipment was also a problem. Its vehicles would not all move at the same tempo and Peiper's armoured spike was likely to become distended and lose its cohesion at the height of the battle's chaos. In short, the role of this Kampfgruppe was to act as a can opener, to reach the Meuse at Amay and to push on to Antwerp. On the plains overlooking the Meuse valley, the Tiger IIs would only feel at ease and deploy their qualities.

Kampfgruppe Sandig

Obersturmbannführer Sandig was 33 years old and had previously been an NCO. He was very hard on his men and applied, to the letter, the adage that sweat spares blood. His battlegroup was formed of:

- SS-Panzergrenadier-Regiment 2, the No. 2 Infantry Regiment minus the 3rd Battalion detached to Peiper
- An Artillery Abteilung, this was the artillery battalion that will bludgeon the small town of Stavelot
- An SS-Flak-Abteilung (anti-aircraft battalion).

Composed mainly of infantrymen, the formation's mission was to follow KG Peiper and to ensure the protection of the armoured point's supplies.

Kampfgruppe Hansen

Obersturmbannführer Max Hansen was 36 years old, making him the oldest commander of the battlegroups. He was adored by his men because he was always in contact with the front line in their company, which had earned him nine injuries. He had under his command:

- SS-Panzergrenadier-Regiment 1
- Panzerjäger-Abteilung, the tank hunters; twenty-one Jagdpanzer IV/70 and StuG, in addition to eleven PAK 40 anti-tank guns (7.5cm)
- Artillery, including the 10.5cm Feldhaubitze (howitzer)
- Twenty-four Nebelwerfer (German equivalent of Stalin's organs)
- A company of pioneers

Kampfgruppe Hansen also had to reach the Meuse at Huy and then drive towards Antwerp. It would be made famous thanks to the images filmed by the propaganda company showing the fighting in the ambush of Poteau, a hamlet between Vielsalm and St. Vith.

Kampfgruppe Knittel

SS-Sturmbannführer Gustav Knittel was the lowest ranking of the four group leaders, and was only 30 years old. His experience of the reconnaissance troops was considerable, having never left the unit, and he had been brought up in the seraglio. The 'Schnelle Gruppe Knittel' was composed as follows:

Knittel had to follow Peiper closely. (*Public domain*)

- SS-Panzer-Aufklärungs-Abteilung 1. The reconnaissance battalion
- A battery of Feldhaubitzen, 10.5cm (10.5cm howitzer)
- A Kompanie SS-Panzer-Pionier (Combat Engineer Company)

This Kampfgruppe was an almost entirely motorised unit, being heavily armed and well equipped with semi-tracks and light armour. Its mission was to follow Max Hansen's Kampfgruppe, overtaking it if necessary, and to arrive at the Meuse as quickly as possible in Huy and its surroundings, in order to capture the bridges intact. The Commander of the 'Leibstandarte', Wilhelm Mohnke, would modify the order of attack of the 'Schnelle Gruppe' and would lead the Knittel column in the Peiper silage to support it. It is this unit that would be responsible, in large part, for the atrocities committed on civilians in Trois-Ponts and Stavelot, as well as in the martyred hamlets of Parfondruy, Ster and Renardmont.

Mission Impossible for KG Peiper?

The first objective assigned to Peiper and his men was to secure a crossing point on the Meuse, more precisely at Ombret-Rausa, near Huy. Ironically, the Waffen-SS route almost followed the line of an ancient Roman road. The breakthrough had to be quick and decisive in order to renew the element of surprise; the main ingredient of the Blitzkrieg tactics which had been the great success in the beginning of the war. The SS officer was instructed to achieve this result within 24 hours of the start of the offensive.

The axis of attack of the Panzers passed through Losheim, Poteau, Ligneuville, Stavelot, Trois-Ponts, Werbomont and Ouffet. Oberstleutnant Friedrich Freiherr von der Heydte's paratroopers and SS-Obersturmbannführer Otto Skorzeny's commandos, including detachments of soldiers dressed in GI uniforms and fluent in American slang, were responsible for providing support. Their task was to support the Kampfgruppe columns by disrupting the enemy's rear, in an operation codenamed *Greif*.

Peiper's target was the Amay bridge, built by the US engineers. (*NARA*)

As we can see, everything had been carefully thought out by the OKW. However, it must be noted that times had changed and that four years had passed since May 1940 and the fateful Panzer breakthrough at Sedan. The Allies now had almost total control of the air, important armoured and anti-tank resources, as well as logistics which, although not perfect, managed to supply millions of combatants as well as the liberated populations of Western Europe. If Peiper and his Kampfgruppe possessed superior weaponry, the element of surprise and a formidable sense of tactics, these were their only assets. The mission can therefore be described as difficult and risky. The SS-Obersturmbannführer and his men were in a race against time, with every minute lost diminishing their chances of completing their objective.

The Expertise of SS-Obersturmbannführer Joachim Peiper

SS-Obersturmbannführer Joachim Peiper was only 29 years old when he received the delicate mission of leading the German offensive. Having joined the Allgemeine SS at the age of 18, he was spotted by Heinrich Himmler, who encouraged him to take up a career as an officer. After graduating as an officer in 1936, he joined the 'Leibstandarte', which was then a regiment-sized Führer's escort organisation, under the command of a loyal follower of the first dictator, a certain Sepp Dietrich. Initially a praetorian guard, the unit grew to become an independent motorised regiment that cut its teeth during the Polish campaign. Peiper did not take part in the operation, having been appointed as Himmler's aide-de-camp in 1938, but finally received his baptism of fire during the French campaign. After a brief return to Himmler, Peiper took part in various operations in Russia. His dazzling career was facilitated by the benevolence of SS-Reichsführer Himmler, and after several heroic and ruthless actions, he was appointed head of SS-Pz-Rgt 1 in November 1943. Until then, he had only commanded armoured infantry units.

Destroyed on the Eastern Front, the 'Leibstandarte', which had in the meantime become the SS-Pz-Div, was sent to Belgium in the spring of 1944 to be replenished. Peiper participated with his Panzer-Regiment in the first battles of his division in Normandy, before being evacuated to a field hospital with jaundice. The illness allowed him to be sent back to the rear before things really turned sour on the front and the last survivors had to escape from the Falaise pocket. Peiper did not return to his unit until early October 1944.[15]

Stationed in Westphalia, SS-Pz-Rgt 1 and the rest of the division were reinforced. Peiper himself admitted that the recruits he was given were of good quality, despite the state of decay in Germany at this point in the war. He added:

> *We received many tanks straight from the assembly lines. Nevertheless, the regiment was supposed to have two battalions, one equipped with Panzer IVs and the other with Panthers. We did not have enough tanks, so I organised my battalion with a mixture of two Panzer IV and two Panther companies. To compensate for the shortage of tanks, my regiment was later reinforced with a Tiger tank battalion, which was previously a corps unit. Thus, the regiment eventually consisted of a mixed Panther and Panzer IV battalion, a Tiger tank battalion and an SS battalion without tanks.*[16]

Three weeks before the Ardennes offensive, Peiper's regiment was transferred to an army reserve 12 kilometres east of Düren, north of Euskirchen. Like the other unit commanders, Peiper was not officially informed of the impending offensive until 14 December. However, he suspected something as early as 11 December after Fritz Kraemer, the chief of staff of the 6. Panzer-Armee, came to him with a bizarre request: '*How long would it take a Panzer Regiment to cover 80 km at night?*' Peiper wanted to give a pragmatic answer and, after completing the test himself in a tank, answered: '*If I have a free road assigned to me, I can cover 80 km in one night. Of course, with a whole division, that's a different matter.*' Peiper, having a clue but no certainty, tried to improve the level of his crews' training by making them drive over hilly terrain and on icy roads. The training could not proceed far, as the enemy was close by and the battle for the Hürtgen Forest was still raging, so the formations of the 6. Panzer-Armee were always on the alert. Worse still, no advance reconnaissance could be carried out, as their presence in the Eifel was strictly forbidden.

An armoured division on the move can be seen as a long snake with several steel-capped heads. These were the various Kampfgruppen of the division. Behind them came the artillery and the countless trucks of its logistical and administrative train. This second wave, essential to the success of the first, was the body of the snake, with a soft, poorly protected belly. If it was attacked and disarticulated, the heads, as fierce as they could be, would die of starvation. This was the stark reality that would eventually cost the 6. Panzer-Armee its victory.

Peiper's sinister reputation was established after he commanded his armoured infantry battalion on the Eastern Front. His men were ferocious and used flamethrowers systematically to destroy villages. (*NARA*)

Chapter 5

Fate is on the Move

The Build-Up to the Battle

On 13 December, mysterious marching orders were distributed. There was no mention of an imminent offensive, only the routes and assembly areas. It was therefore for Peiper and his men to leave for an unknown future in the assembly area allocated to the 1. SS-Pz-Div in the heart of the triangle formed by the entities of Marmegen–Blankenheimerdorf–Schmidtheim, the advanced elements of the divisional unit being in Dahlem. Strict precautions were taken to maintain absolute secrecy, with instructions only being given to the troops just before they were to move. The advance was made in

Final preparations for the assault are made. (*Rights reserved*)

complete radio silence and on a dark night when only the *Notek* could be used.[1] The route was marked by simple yellow arrows on which no mention of the unit was made. Peiper's regiment began to move out at 19:00 on 13 December and arrived at its assigned area by 10:00 the next day. The advance was uneventful, the clouds being far too thick to allow any air operations in the area. The crews had a hard time of it:

> *After the advance on Blieshein, we had to shelter our tanks in the assembly area in the forest of Schmidtheim, erase the marks of their tracks and camouflage them against aerial observation. We used bush branches for sleeping and as a windbreak. We spent the time freezing and thinking about the action to come. Nobody knew anything. Where were we going to go? There was absolute secrecy about the operation.*

Another soldier described how his teeth were chattering and no fire was allowed to keep warm. Just a small fire of twigs underneath his reconnaissance vehicle to keep the engine warm was allowed.[2]

The Little Roads of the Ardennes

SS-Oberführer Wilhelm Mohnke commanded the 1. SS-Panzer-Division 'Leibstandarte SS Adolf Hitler'. (*NARA*)

On the evening of 14 December, Peiper and the other commanders were summoned to the divisional command post, where SS-Oberführer Wilhelm Mohnke unveiled the plan of the offensive and read out the detailed orders from I. SS-Panzer-Korps assigning the various routes. D-Day was set for the morning of 16 December.[3] The mission assigned to Peiper's detachment was: *'The gepanzerte Gruppe*[4] *Peiper will attack on 16 December at hour X in the Losheim–Losheimergraben sector and break through the American front. Initial objective: capture and hold the bridge over the Meuse south of Liège.'* The armoured regiment was instructed to conduct the battle without regard to its flanks or to the development of the battle on either side of its axis of attack, and to exploit the speed of its Panzers in order to reach the Meuse.[5] Each unit leader received a marked map with the routes they had to follow. Peiper's route passed through Schmidtheim – Dahlem – Kronenburg – Scheid – Losheim – Losheimergraben – Hünningen – Honsfeld – Möderscheid – Schoppen – Ondenval – Thirimont – Ligneuville – Stavelot – Trois-Ponts – Werbomont – Ouffet – Seny – Tinlot – Strée to finally arrive at the edge of the Meuse in Huy.[6] The route needed to be covered in a day to guarantee the rapid crossing of the river, the only real obstacle before Antwerp.[7]

The young Peiper earned his stripes on the Eastern Front and was close to Himmler. (*Rights reserved*)

An SS-Panzer-Shutze ready to fight. (*NARA*)

Peiper soon realised that his roads were difficult and could not help but envy those of his neighbours, which he considered to be much better. He immediately pointed out that the roads he would have to use were more suitable for bicycles than for Panzers. He was told, however, that these were the Führer's orders and that he had to follow the route he had been given. Clearly, this last point was very problematic. Peiper had in his column 70-ton behemoths, almost 4 metres wide and 10 metres long if one takes into account the 88-mm gun that equipped the Tiger II tanks. These machines were heavy tanks with fragile mechanics that required special care. They were very different from the Panther and Panzer IVs, the medium tanks they were forced to fight alongside due to the lack of available equipment. The Tiger tanks were brought to the front according to rules specifically established to limit their wear, meaning they needed to advance at a constant speed with regular maintenance stops.

Order and Manner

The art of the commander of an armoured column is to arrange his resources in such a way as to adapt them to the mission he has to accomplish. Peiper had been ordered to carry out a surprise attack on the bridges of the Meuse. He therefore needed to think primarily of combining speed and strength, and the staggering of his column reflected the content of his mission. As soon as he received his instructions, Peiper described how he sat down and thought about how he would organise his various elements:

The SPWs led the assault alongside the Panthers. (*Rights reserved*)

> *I decided that my column would be approximately 25 kilometres long and that the vehicles would advance at an intermediate speed. It was impossible for the vehicles at the rear to overtake those at the front because of the bad roads. Consequently, all my combat elements had to be placed at the front of the column. In order to have maximum speed and power, I decided that my armoured halftracks would advance as fast as possible until they met resistance, and then the tanks would arrive to destroy this resistance, which would then allow the halftracks to resume their advance. I felt that if all went well, I would only need my Panzer IVs and Panthers to get through the mountainous area*[8] *and reach the Meuse with a tank company. Then I could use my heavy Tigers afterwards.*[9]

For the first two days of the battle, the result of Peiper's reflections was validated by the facts given in the above order.

The *Spitze* [Point]

This had to open the road and push through any resistance with vigour. It therefore consisted mainly of tanks and a small engineering element to clear any minefields detected. This point was placed under the command of SS-Obersturmführer Werner Sternebeck.

- 1 Zug[10], 6. Komp/SS-Pz-Rgt 1 consisting of five Panzer IV
- ½ Zug, 1. Komp/SS-Pz-Rgt 1 with two Panthers
- 1 Gruppe, 9. Komp (Panzer-Pionier) Pz-Rgt 1 (mounted on SPW)

The *Spitzen* Kompanien

The advanced companies were mainly composed of armoured infantrymen, the latter mounted in armoured half-tracks. The infantrymen dismounted and their vehicles, armed with a machine gun or cannon, supported the assault. Hauptsturmführer Georg Preuss commanded this second part of the column:

- 1 Zug, 10. Komp SS-Pz-Gren-Rgt 2
- 1 Zug, 9. Komp SS-Pz-Rgt 1 (minus the Gruppe inserted in the *Spitze*)
- 1 Zug, 10. Komp SS-Pz-Gren-Rgt 2
- 1 Zug, 12. Komp SS-Pz-Gren-Rgt 2
- 1 Zug, 10. Komp SS-Pz-Gren-Rgt 2

The Stab of Gepanzerte Gruppe Peiper

Next came the column command echelon, where Peiper took his place alongside his two main commanders, SS-Sturmbannführer Werner Poetschke at the head of I. Pz-Rgt 1 and SS-Sturmbannführer Jupp Diefenthal commanding III. (Gep)/SS-Panzer-Grenadier-Regiment 2.

The Main Body of the Battle

This staff would be deployed as needed according to events.

Most of the rest of the available tanks were here:

- 1.Komp I. SS-Pz-Rgt 1 (a company equipped with Panthers)
- 11. Komp III. SS- Pz-Gren-Rgt 2
- 6. Komp II. SS-Pz-Rgt 1 (a company equipped with Panzer IVs)
- 9. Komp SS-Pz-Pi-Rgt 1 (the balance of the Panzer-Pioniere)
- 7. Komp II. SS-Pz-Rgt 1 (the second Panzer IV company)
- 10. (Flak)/SS-Pz-Rgt 1 (the air defence elements)
- 3. Komp SS-Pz-Pi-Abt 1
- 2. Komp I. SS-Pz-Rgt 1 (the second Panther company)
- 13, Schwere Komp III. Pz-Gren-Rgt 2 (the support company of the infantry Abteilung accompanying Peiper)
- 12. Komp III. SS-Pz-Gren-Rgt 2
- 9. Komp III. SS-Pz-Gren-Rgt 2
- schwere SS-Pz-Abt 501 (the forty-five Tiger IIs)
- Flak-Sturm-Abteilung 84 (Sf.)
- II. SS-Pz-Artillery-Rgt 1

The Train

Next came the logistical and medical elements.[11] The layout of Peiper's column reflected his mission, the configuration of the terrain and the means at his disposal. The SS officer hoped to move quickly and to alternate between armoured and infantry vehicles, depending on the resistance encountered. In the end, this was a rather basic vision that did not give him the means to play the joint configuration card. For Peiper, the frontal shock should have allowed him to win the day. It is true that the initial breakthrough needed to be achieved by the infantry. His mission was to exploit the situation quickly: in theory, the faster he advanced, the more surprise he would be able to achieve.

The Tigers were relegated to the end of the column, which was also a wise choice. Their guns, with their long-range engagement capability, were of no use in the highly compartmentalised Ardennes terrain. Peiper intended to use them in the second phase of his advance, beyond the Meuse into the Hesbaye plains, where the view was largely unobstructed. In this area, the Tiger's long range, which was capable of destroying a Sherman at 2,000 metres without the latter being able to retaliate, was also a tactical choice that could seem judicious. It seems to us, however, that the original sin lay in this arrangement. The logistic supply train was behind the heavy tanks, and the speed differential between the medium and heavy tanks caused the column to break up longitudinally. The first elements would advance too fast for the next element to keep up. Peiper did not need them for the first phase of his operation, so this was apparently not a problem. However, his support train was too far behind and he would not have access to it. Tanks and infantry were still the rulers of the battle, but they could not do anything without supplies and maintenance…

Chapter 6

The Difficult Breakthrough

The Failure of the 12. Volks-Grenadier-Division

It was the 12. VGD which was to open the road to the Peiper column. According to its leader's report, it was in a much worse state than the I. SS-Panzer-Korps staff had thought. The division had only been withdrawn from the front on the night of 2/3 December to be placed in army group reserve behind the lines of the 7. Armee, having suffered considerable losses. Its infantry units had lost two thirds of their strength, while its artillery batteries were still more or less in order. However, the losses had been very heavy in the ranks of its artillery observers, which would make its fire settings very inaccurate. Close support weapons (machine guns, mortars and anti-tank guns) were 90% missing, and it only had six assault guns left.

It was the 12. VGD's role to open the road for the Peiper column. (*Rights reserved*)

Generalmajor Engel was only informed on 11 December of the offensive in which his division was to take part. It was at this moment that he learned the content of his mission: to break through the front at Losheimergraben and then attack on both sides of the Bütgenbach–Malmedy road. Depending on the course of the battle, it would then have to move northwards to the Verviers area to protect the right flank of the armoured formations. The unit commanders of the 12. VGD asked to postpone the attack because of the poor state of the troops. Hitler refused, citing both military and political reasons. Every effort was made to get the division back into fighting shape and, in what Engel describes as a surprisingly short time, 3,000 new recruits and 500 rehabilitated soldiers joined the unit. The new arrivals

The 394th Infantry Regiment of the 99th Infantry Division received the main force of the German attack. (*NARA*)

were, in fact, soldiers withdrawn from service in the rear and were very poorly trained. Although infantry weapons arrived quickly, the lack of anti-tank guns was not addressed. Moreover, no assault guns were added to the six that were recovered from the previous front and refurbished. Meanwhile, minimal training was provided for the fighters.

The first troops of the division moved in the night of 14/15 December to relieve the 277. VGD. The only thing Engel knew was that he had the 99th Infantry Division in front of him and that its position was very extensive.[1] It was the 394th Infantry Regiment of this division that would receive the main force of the German attack.

Colonel Don Riley, in command of the 394th Infantry Regiment, placed his first two battalions in the front line, the third being in divisional reserve on his right flank to the south. His front was very strongly extended over 5.5 kilometres. The extreme south of its sector was held by the Regimental Intelligence and Reconnaissance Platoon, covering the Lanzerath road. Since the regiment had been in line, apart from the occasional patrols and artillery fire, the front had been relatively quiet and no one, from the rank and file to the general, had any idea of what was going on on the German side.[2]

Engel's plan was to employ two attack groups deployed on either side of the Losheim–Büllingen road, Fusilier Regiment 27 on the right and Grenadier Regiment 48 on the left. His intention was to reach the Hürringen and Hünningen Heights west of the Gerolstein Forest. He deduced from what he knew of the enemy's position that if he managed to occupy these high points, his breakthrough would be successful, as this is where the rear of the American artillery batteries was located.[3]

German artillery opened fire at 05:30 on the American positions. Staff Sergeant John Hilliard of C Company, I/394th IR, recalled:

> *It was the heaviest artillery barrage of the war and I am sure no one would want to experience it again. There was fire and smoke everywhere. The tops of the trees were hit and pieces of trunks were flying in all directions. The Germans were carrying out a rolling*

The assault began with a proper artillery preparation. (*Rights reserved*)

> *barrage, shells were hitting the ground in front of our positions. The enemy gunners would lengthen their fire with each salvo and in this way move their bombardment area over and behind our positions. They repeated this tactic continuously and hit their targets. This continuous and intensive barrage caused a terrible shock to the nervous system and made it difficult for individuals to react in a reasonable way. Many of our men went mad and left their shelters to be killed or maimed.*[4]

From the German point of view, the attack started well. The troops started their advance from 06:00 and by 09:00, Fusilier Regiment 27 had reported the capture of Losheim and announced its deployment on both sides of the railway line. However, they soon found themselves involved in fierce fighting with several American outposts, and the attack began to lag considerably. The US defensive sector was apparently very well prepared with barbed wire, log barriers and mines. Around noon, Grenadier Regiment 48 announced that it was stopped in front of Losheimergraben, where the Americans had transformed the houses into entrenched positions and were resisting tenaciously.

Peiper's Impatience

The 3. Fallschirmjäger-Division attacked on the southern flank. (*Rights reserved*)

The American resistance was, naturally, not good for Peiper. He was at Engel's headquarters at 05:00, where the reports were gradually coming in and could thus follow the evolution of the fighting and estimate the moment when he would finally be able to unleash his Panthers. He learned that a bridge in No Man's Land had been destroyed the previous autumn by retreating German troops. After it was repaired, the order was given for the artillery of the 12. VGD. However, this was horse-drawn and advanced only very slowly to the point of obstructing the bridge until 19:00. Peiper arrived on the spot at 19:30 and managed to find a way around the bridge via a small path down into the ditch. He then learned that the next bridge on the railway line had also been destroyed and could not be repaired as the engineer formations were unable to reach it. He was next ordered to advance to Lanzerath, where he joined elements of Fallschirmjäger-Regiment 9 of 3. Fallschirmjäger-Division. This unit had attempted to attack through the wood west of Lanzerath towards Honsfeld and was driven back three times. He was ordered to take command of this regiment and to attack.[5]

It was at this moment that Peiper suffered his first losses. SS-Obersturmführer Werner Sternebeck was with his *Spitze* and said:

> *Immediately west of Losheim, the first Panther fell into a minefield and was lost for the rest of the operation. After the pioneers had removed the mines, the advance was cautiously resumed. By this time the sun was declining, uncertainty was growing, we knew nothing about the enemy. There was a second explosion. The second Panther had just hit the next minefield 500 metres west of Losheim. Once again the mines had to be detected and removed. This took some time. Our two Panthers which we thought we were using as battle rams were lost for the rest of the operation, without having had any contact with the enemy. Immediately south-east of Merlscheid, at an open road obstacle, my Panzer was startled and after a bang, it stopped. It too was out of action.*[6]

In total Peiper claimed to have lost five tanks and the same number of armoured vehicles before reaching Lanzerath at midnight, without encountering a single GI.

Building a bridge took a long time. (*NARA*)

The Road Opens Up Before Peiper

The 3. FJD was ordered to advance roughly along the southern shoulder of the Honsfeld road. The sector was defended and included the northern half of the sector of the 14th Cavalry Group (CG), which had installed half of its resources there by putting one of its two reconnaissance squadrons, the 18th Cavalry Reconnaissance Squadron (CRS) in the first line. Lanzerath was defended to the south by these cavalrymen, while the heights north-west of the village were held by the Regimental Intelligence and Reconnaissance Platoon 394th Regiment of the 99th ID. This platoon was on the south wing, behind the regiment's main line of resistance. It was, in fact, in reserve. The pressure exerted during 16 December on the I/396th IR and II/394th IR caused them to withdraw, which finally allowed Peiper to advance westwards into the village. The IR Platoon stood up to the paratroopers, who were inexperienced in infantry combat. The paratroopers launched three frontal attacks, each time stopped by the .30s of the IR Platoon GIs. At the end of the day, the novice paratroopers attacked again, this time from the flanks, and overran the dominant positions of the village held by the GIs. On the other hand, the III/394th IR

The III/394th IR had no choice but to maintain contact with neighbouring units and abandon the heights north-west of Lanzerath. (*NARA*)

had no choice but to maintain contact with the neighbouring units and to abandon the heights north-west of Lanzerath.

There, the SS officer conferred with the Oberst commanding Fallschirmjäger-Regiment 9 (FJR 9) from whom he obtained information on the enemy's position. According to the Fallschirmjäger leader, the woods were heavily fortified with prepared pillboxes and mines on the road, all of which had blocked his advance during the day. Peiper was furious when he learned that no officer had personally recognised the American positions and decided to lead the breakthrough himself by taking command of an Abteilung of the regiment. At 01:00 on 17 December, Peiper convened a council of war with the commanders of the units attached to his battle group. He ordered his troops to make a breakthrough at 04:00. An armoured spike took the lead, consisting of two Panther tanks in front, followed by SPWs and the rest of the Panthers and Panzer IVs. The column passed Buchholz without encountering any resistance. Peiper recalled: *'One kilometre north-west of Honsfeld we received small arms fire, but it did not worry us. Although it caused a small delay, it allowed the rear vehicles to close in.'*[7] Peiper's account, however, does not give a clear picture of what actually happened at Honsfeld where the American resistance was surprised.

Peiper's armoured *Spitze* (point) penetrated Honsfeld. (*NARA*)

During 16 December, the very extensive lines of the 18th CRS were breached. The 14th CG brought its second squadron, the 32nd CRS, online, where it set up a first defensive screen stretching from Manderfeld to Andler. This collection line allowed the crushed elements of the 18th CRS to withdraw and reorganise. The pressure increased and 32nd CRS was forced to withdraw. As part of this manoeuvre, his A Troop arrived at Honsfeld on 16 December shortly after 21:00, where it found a captain of the 99th Infantry Division in charge of the Rest Center[8] of his division. The American officer set up a defensive line with what he could gather: resting GIs, runaways and some Tank Destroyers of various units. He asked Lieutenant Reppa, the head of A Troop, to reinforce the line. Reppa set up his vehicles in the village while the infantrymen took up positions to the south and south-west of the village. All the houses in the village were filled with GIs. As Peiper was about to unleash his forces to the west, the defenders of Honsfeld were preparing for the shock. All night long, the small village was crossed by fleeing American vehicles.[9]

Fierce Resistance in Honsfeld

In mid-December the famous actress and singer Marlene Dietrich was about to give a concert at the GI's rest centre in Honsfeld. At the sound of the approaching offensive, she evacuated to the rear of the front, leaving the area to another Dietrich.[10]

A German paratrooper, Rudi Frühbeisser, wrote a book in which he described the fighting his unit witnessed during this period. The book includes his version of events following the serious argument that broke out between Peiper and the commander of FJR 9 over the progress of the attack. (It should be noted that although the account is a very useful source, Frühbeisser's habit of often talking about himself in the third person can sometimes lead to confusion. However, whenever the extracts have been reproduced here, they appear in their original format):

> *Our regimental commander, who had already been a staff colonel for years, did not hide his opinion. For the SS, it was a matter of taking our 1st battalion on the march at all times. But our regimental commander only agreed to this to ensure the safety of the paratroopers mounted on the tanks until they crossed the Büllingen Forest. At 06:00, the 1st Battalion was alerted and sat down on the approaching tanks. Part of the 1st Company, almost all of them 'old men', were stationed around their leader at the turret. Then the race began. We took the same route. When the road forked, we signalled to the commander that the machine gun was on the right in the forest.*
>
> *At a crossroads we turned left and the journey continued to thunderous applause. After a while, we approached the fork in the road to the left in the direction of Holzheim. The tank stopped. Some of us sat down and walked towards the fork in the road, ensuring our safety. Up ahead, on the road, the passing of vehicles could be clearly heard. The journey continued. Fortunately, it was still dark. In daylight, the vehicles, American trucks and tanks, would have seen that a royal tiger was following them. A new fork in the road came into view, leading to the village of Hünningen on the right. Near the lonely house, several*

jeeps were parked. Quickly, some of them dismounted and entered the house. The men of a staff were preparing to leave, but the Americans would go to Germany as prisoners. Among them were two captains and some lieutenants.

The journey continued cautiously with our Königstiger which, with its 8.8 gun, was heading for the town of Honsfeld. The tank commander said to his crew over the intercom: "With this bunch of paratroopers I want to go to Liège!" As the town of Honsfeld lay before us in the dawning daylight, our tank stopped. At a sign from our leader, the whole company took position away from the tanks. We immediately entered the houses on the left and right. The Americans were everywhere. Without the company knowing it, we had entered the rest camp of the 99th Infantry Division and the 549th Regiment US.[11] *The Americans were immediately disarmed and their weapons rendered useless. Then they were driven out onto the road. Well, that would be a prize for our commander.*[12]

Frühbeisser's account overlaps perfectly with that of Sergeant George Creel, who commanded an armoured car of the 32nd CRS. He said that the fleeing vehicles were suddenly replaced by a Tiger tank with a large black cross. It seems that the first German

The spoils captured were impressive. (*NARA*)

Paratroopers accompanied the Tigers in the assault. (*NARA*)

elements entered the village by surprise. It was still dark and the noise of the fleeing vehicles covered the arrival of Peiper's tanks. The cavalrymen quickly pulled themselves together, the alert was given through the unit's radio network and 2nd Platoon, who were defending the southern entrances to Honsfeld, opened fire.[13]

Frühbeisser confirmed:

> *Suddenly, as we were climbing back onto the tanks, a shot went off. From almost every window in the village a shower of fire rained down on the paratroopers in the vicinity. Fire was immediately opened up. There was also American fire. And quite a lot! Already the first groups were jumping back to the village. Our tank turns its 88 and fired at a machine gun; direct hit! The first houses were already taken over and the Americans rejected. Many Americans fell under machine gun and rifle fire. Here, too, there were the first losses.*[14]

Casualties accumulated in the German ranks and gave another idea of the fighting spirit of the inexperienced GIs of the 99th Infantry Division reinforced by the cavalrymen of the 32nd CRS:

> *From the ll. staff, Burghardt was mortally wounded by shrapnel in the chest and thigh. In 5. Kompagnie, attacking the locality from the other side with its leader, Lieutenant von Homburg, Gefreiter Heller was shot in the head. When the company medic, Feldmarschall Bär, tried to attend to him, he received a fatal blow to the chest. Obergefreiter Sebald and Obergefreiter Wagenfeld were also killed by shrapnel.*
>
> *Ten other men of the 5. Kompagnie were seriously wounded by shrapnel in the head, chest, neck and mouth. The group leader, Obergefreiter Held of the 6. Kompagnie, was hit in the head. The fight between the houses continued and became more and more difficult. Now a few American Jabos intervened, but they were eliminated by the Wirbelwind and were shot down or driven away. […]*
>
> *American fire also broke out. Artillery fire came from somewhere in the village. Some tanks had already entered the village to support the paratroopers in their fight. Near a tank, Warrant Officer Hoffmann of the 1. Komp received some shrapnel in the foot. The stationary tank offered him good protection. The company medic, Feldwebel Josef Otto, went to the wounded man. Then a grenade exploded next to the tank. Otto collapsed. Corporal Frühbeisser, who was looking through a window in the house opposite, saw his medic fall. He decided to jump out of the window and drag the sergeant behind the Panther and position him behind the undercarriage. Staff Sergeant Otto was blue in the face. He shouted, "Don't sit me down, lay me down, I'm having a heart attack."*
>
> *Frühbeisser unbuttoned his clothes and saw a round hole 1 centimetre below the nipple, from which a little blood was flowing. It had to be right at the heart, Frühbeisser thought. He took out the first-aid kit, which he first had to fetch from under the fire in the street. Suddenly, the tank started up again. Sergeant Otto was now on the road, unprotected. Immediately, an American fired explosive bullets at the man lying in the*

The first days of the assault were characterised by thick fog, which favoured the attackers. (*Public domain*)

road. A Jagdbomber [fighter bomber] *crashed to the ground and the pilot was killed. The Americans continued to fire on the road, causing stones to fly. A large stone hit Frühbeisser's jump helmet and chest. Dazed, he managed to reach Feldwebel Otto and jump back. Once again, he dragged his friend towards the house where he was before. But someone else has already spotted him and targeted him. Next to a pile of wood, Frühbeisser could finally put down his Feldwebel.*

With a few bandages, he made the dressing as tight as possible. Across the meadow, an armoured vehicle with the Red Cross sign arrived. Frühbeisser signalled him to come closer. An SS doctor in a white coat walked alongside and asked what was going on. Frühbeisser briefly explained his injury to the doctor. The doctor signalled the driver to load the wounded man and continued to run to attend to a wounded SS officer. The driver got out of the back and approached. Suddenly a grenade fell next to him and he fell dead.

When Frühbeisser looked into the SPW, several SS men lay inside, their heads bandaged. Together with another fighter, they took Feldwebel Otto into the SPW and lay him on the ground. The grenade fire was getting more and more intense, so all that was left to do was to leave! He climbed into the SPW, sat in the driver's seat (the engine was still running,) put the car in gear, released the handbrake and set off. He passed the house and turned into the street. "If I can get through here", Frühbeisser thought, "I can help the poor guys screaming in the SPW". Shots rang out at the SPW, almost tearing his ears off. Suddenly the firing stopped just before the railway. So Frühbeisser turned around again, which he managed to do after some effort. Again, the Americans fired at the SPW, although it was clearly marked with the red cross sign. Then he chased after a VW which was driving through the village at full speed. The SPW bumped up the hill. But according to Frühbeisser, that was not the road they took. It was the road to Holzheim! Several times, he saw groups of American prisoners being guarded in the field. After stopping, he asked a fellow countryman where an aid post was. The latter pointed to the left-hand fork in the road and shouted: "200 metres! 200 metres!" and pointed in his direction. After 200 metres, a Red Cross flag was seen hanging from a tree.

A few tents were set up at the edge of the forest, under some trees. This was an aid station of the unit to which the SPW belonged. When Frühbeisser looked down from his SPW, an SS doctor asked him: "So, paratrooper, what are you doing with our SPW?" Frühbeisser then explained what happened. The doctor then said to the SS medics who were there: "There you go, you idiots, you should be paratroopers, then you could help yourselves too". The wounded were quickly unloaded. The doctor, at Frühbeisser's request and by way of thanks, then took Feldwebel Otto first. He shook his head at the wound, knowing there was not much more that could be done.[15, 16]

During this odyssey to the rear of the attack, the fighting continued in Honsfeld. The first line of American defence, made up of rearmed GIs, flinched. According to the reports of the 32nd CRS, some Tank Destroyer crews abandoned their tanks and fled without firing a single shot. An assertion to be put into perspective when one reads the report of the engagement of B Company of the 612th Tank Destroyer Battalion:

On 18 December, B Company (plus the 1st Reconnaissance Platoon) was detached from the 23rd Infantry Regiment[17] *and attached to the 99th ID, moving to the vicinity of Honsfeld, Belgium, where it took up a position of preparation. An attack in a south-easterly direction by a large number of tanks and armoured infantry resulted in the destruction of two self-propelled anti-tank guns by 1st Platoon, B Company, and one enemy tank by 2nd Platoon, B Company, before both platoons were overrun by enemy infantry.*[18]

Behind this first line of defence, the cavalrymen were able to resist against the Fallschirmjäger, but the 37-mm guns in their vehicles were no match for the Tiger. The Germans entered the town and the GIs in the houses fled north. The commander of A Troop, 32nd CRS, had only a limited vision of the situation, but realised that he was surrounded by tanks. On the basis of this observation, he ordered a 'state of emergency'.[19] He only managed to gather forty-three men with him.[20] In other words, A Troop had just lost the essential part of its strike force.

Back in Honsfeld, where some shots were still being fired, Frühbeisser could only see the damage:

The fighting in Honsfeld was hard. More than 150 Americans were trapped in a meadow. The loot of vehicles, armoured infantry fighting vehicles and guns was large. The loot of fuel and tankers was even more important. The village was in a terrible state: Americans, paratroopers and SS grenadiers had fallen in the streets. Vehicles were on fire, a German

The SS committed their first acts of violence in the assault, killing three civilians and shooting fifteen prisoners in Honsfeld. (*NARA*)

> *tank had also been destroyed. At the intersection of Heppenbach and Büllingen there was an anti-aircraft tank whose crew has been burnt.*[21]

The FJR 9 counted thirteen killed and sixty-four wounded in its ranks for the capture of Honsfeld. As for Peiper, he provided further details about the American equipment

The Germans took the shoes and socks of the dead GIs. One of the corpses was crushed by Peiper's tanks: the body sank so deeply into the mud that it was not found until work was carried out in the area in autumn 1990. (*NARA*)

that had fallen into his hands: fifty reconnaissance vehicles, including half-tracks, eighty 2.5-ton GMCs and between fifteen and sixteen anti-tank guns.[22] The SS also committed their first acts of violence here, killing three civilians and shooting fifteen prisoners.[23]

Fruitful Diversions to Büllingen

With the first US lines finally broken through, Peiper now hoped to advance towards the Meuse with little or no opposition. He was already two days behind the precise timing of the operation, but the Kamfgruppe's massive wagon was already running out of fuel because of traffic jams. Military intelligence had informed the assault units that there was a large American petrol depot in Büllingen (Bullange). Peiper explained that he advanced without difficulty to Büllingen, crushing twelve American L5 liaison aircraft in the process. The ground crew resisted with only their small arms. Normally the town was on the road of the neighbouring division, the 12. SS-Pz-Div. But he knew that the latter was having difficulties and could not advance. The road was therefore free for him and he could take the route without the risk of causing a huge traffic jam.[24]

The diversions allowed him to capture 200,000 litres of fuel in Büllingen, and he used fifty of his prisoners to refuel all his tanks. Peiper later said:

> *It was a lucky capture because from the time we reached Losheim we burned in 25 kilometres what we would normally consume to cover 50, thanks to the mountainous terrain of the Eifel. Shortly after capturing the town, the American artillery opened up a barrage at 09:30 hours on 17 December, causing us some casualties. From there we moved south-west*

The fighting also took its toll on the German troops. (*Rights reserved*)

One Flak Panzer IV 3.7cm Möbel was lost at Honsfeld. It is seen here being inspected after the fighting. (*NARA*)

KG Peiper advanced effortlessly to Büllingen, crushing twelve American L5 liaison aircraft in the process. (*NARA*)

> *through Möderscheid. The only difficulty was the road through the woods, where several of our vehicles got bogged down. We surprised the small US garrison at Möderscheid.*

Peiper believed that now the road ahead was free, he would hardly meet any resistance. '*At all times we ran into jeeps that wanted to take our route from adjacent roads that apparently did not realise we had penetrated so deeply.*'[25]

Chapter 7

A Trail of Blood from Büllingen to Baugnez

On the way to Baugnez

One of the most resounding massacres perpetrated by KG Peiper took place at Baugnez, although Peiper does not mention it in his interrogation: *'A short distance north of Thirimont, our lead tank fired on a convoy following the road from Malmedy to Ligneuville. [...] Eleven to fifteen of their trucks were destroyed and we got through the convoy with some difficulty, then pushed on towards Ligneuville.'*[1]

In fact, on 17 December 1944, the main column of B Battery, 285th Field Artillery Observation Battalion, 152 men strong, was on its way to St. Vith to support the

The Panzer IVs followed in the rear of Peiper's armoured column. (*Rights reserved via BWM*)

The village of Baugnez was the scene of a tragedy that would forever live in people's minds. (*NARA*)

operations of the VIII Corps. On the way, at about 00:45, it inadvertently came across the tip of KG Peiper. Sergeant Kenneth F. Ahrens was in the fourth vehicle of the column at the time of the fatal encounter:

> *We were moving on the road between Malmedy and St. Vith going south. About 10 kilometres from St. Vith we were stopped by mortar and machine gun fire from the east. The fire was so intense that we had to get out of our vehicles. As soon as I got out of the jeep I crawled into a ditch along the road. Finding that this was not sufficient protection, the men with me crossed the road and we crawled back along a house. The whole column was stopped. Then we heard the tanks coming. The first tank that came near us was a Panther. At this point the men were forced to throw down their weapons, as we had no way of fighting the German tanks. Four or five more German tanks then passed us. The Germans on these tanks were gesturing to us to keep our hands up and get back on the road. The Panzer-grenadiere infantry had us completely surrounded.*[2]

Although the Americans were visibly distraught, the firing continued until Peiper himself arrived. In his version of events, he ordered a ceasefire:

> *This column was travelling south at high speed. I saw the first vehicle in the convoy disappear behind the curve to the south. I saw the last vehicle at the crossroads, but more*

trucks and jeeps were still coming. My forward point vehicles had opened fire. I gave the order to cease firing several times as I was annoyed at having lost so much time already. Also, I was annoyed that these beautiful trucks, which we would need so much, were being strafed. It took about two minutes before my order was understood by all. With that I ordered to continue driving at high speed. I then got into the vehicle of Sturmbannführer Werner Poetschke and ordered him to send a radio message to the division. He was to report that the enemy was leaving Malmedy, that they were retreating to the south and south-west and that we had reached the main road south of Malmedy.[3]

All in all, Peiper's stop there was short, barely five minutes. He did not have time to organise the liquidation of the prisoners. Obsessed by the time already lost since the previous day, he decided to continue forward, meaning what happened next was carried out in his absence. Sergeant Kenneth F. Ahrens continued:

As we were standing in this field with our hands up, a tracked vehicle stopped in the road about 25 metres from us. An officer or non-commissioned officer was on top of this vehicle. There were also two other tracked vehicles in front of this vehicle. The German on top of the vehicle drew his pistol and, as if he was on exercise, he fired into the group, aiming deliberately. I then noticed about 3 metres away from me in the front row that one of the men in my battery was slumped on the ground with a bullet through his head. As I looked towards this German, another shot went off. A few yards from the first victim another man in my battery fell to the ground, shot through the head. Immediately after the two pistol shots, the machine guns opened fire on us. I spun around and fell face down on the ground. No sooner was I lying on the ground than one of the bullets from the machine guns hit me in the back. The machine gun fire from these two or three vehicles continued for half an hour, sweeping us with criss-crossing bursts. After the firing stopped, these vehicles continued on to St. Vith. The other vehicles coming from the crossroads would riddle us with bullets as they passed us laying in the field. This went on for maybe half an hour, an hour.[4]

It is difficult to determine what actually triggered the shooting of the prisoners. In his book *Massacres en Ardenne*, the historian Matthieu Longue lists no less than seven different theories.[5] It seems that the most probable is that an attempt to escape by some of the GIs caused all the men in the field to be shot. In a report written for the Historical Division European Command after the Dachau trial, Peiper had a similar opinion on the origin of the massacre:

During the trial against the 1. SS-Panzer-Regiment, one of the eighty survivors of the group of prisoners stated: "the shooting started when I had almost reached the edge of the forest". During the same trial, the American prosecution tried to prove that the US POWs in the field were shot down voluntarily by a well-prepared action. As evidence, the prosecution called Lieutenant Larry as a witness. This officer was standing in the

The main column of B Battery, 285th Field Artillery Observation Battalion was surprised in Baugnez. (*NARA*)

At Baugnez, prisoners were gathered in a field where they were to be executed. (*NARA*)

field among the prisoners. Without intending to deduce any facts, the following can be stated: the deposition of one of the eighty survivors certifies that the shooting began when the group that had remained compact up to that point was visibly fleeing. This version appears to be more reliable than the version of Lieutenant Larry, who after a delay of two years recognised a German soldier who was passing by in a tank, who could only be seen for a few seconds, and who was voluntarily responsible for the shooting of the POWs.[6]

Already punishable, the Baugnez affair was not limited to the shooting of prisoners who were trying or not trying to escape. It ended with the systematic killing of the wounded. Private Gustav Sprenger arrived in an Sd.Kfz. 251 just after the event. He explained what happened after the first shooting:

Our SPW arrived at the crossroads between 13:00 and 14:00. I saw between 50 and 80 prisoners lying in a field to the right of the road. I stopped my vehicle opposite Beutner's on the other side of the road. I saw a group of officers and soldiers in this field. The prisoners were bathed in blood. Then Beutner went to our vehicle and ordered us to enter the field and finish off the prisoners who still showed signs of life.[7]

This second act of the tragedy is a war crime that is not open to interpretation.

It should be noted that the massacre of eighty-four prisoners at Baugnez was not the only one perpetrated by the 1. SS-Panzer-Division, to which must be added the fifteen at Honsfeld, seven at La Gleize and eight at Ligneuville. The frequency of these crimes, which all took place in less than a week, at a peak time of the breakthrough, suggests that this was a deliberate intention of the command.

The Orders

Sepp Dietrich declared on 22 March 1946 that he had been instructed to act with brutality, but stated that he had never personally given an order to shoot prisoners of war or civilians. (*NARA*)

When such abuses are committed, two different readings of the facts can take place. On the one hand, combatants may have decided to commit crimes on their own, on the other hand, the command may have given the order. In the case of the *Wacht am Rhein* offensive, the ambiguity of the instructions given through the hierarchy was undoubtedly the starting point. The first link in the chain of command was Adolf Hitler himself. Indeed, just before the offensive, he harangued his generals and specified: '*Terror must be fought with terror. All resistance must be broken without* mercy.'[8] For Priess, leader of the I. SS-Panzer-Korps, this terror referred to a response to the Allied aerial bombardments. This is confirmed by Mohnke when he evoked the spirit of the Führer, who would have specified that the fight must be carried out '*without human inhibition and that all must remember the victims of the terror bombings*'.[9]

Just before the offensive, Adolf Hitler's orders were read to the troops and are open to an interpretation that urges savagery: '*The decisive hour for the German people has arrived, and the imminent offensive must be won at all costs. The fighter must be tough and reckless; the troops must act with brutality and show no human feeling. A wave of fear must precede the troops, and the enemy's resistance must be broken by terror.*'[10]

The sector in which the abuses were mainly committed was under the responsibility of the 6. Panzer-Armee, under the command of Generaloberst (or SS-Oberstgruppenführer) Sepp Dietrich. In his affidavit of 22 March 1946, he stated that he was instructed to act brutally, but claimed that he personally never gave the order to shoot prisoners of war or civilians, although he did order that all resistance be broken by terror.[11] It is possible that he did not make such a commitment, but at his staff conference on 14 December 1944, when asked: '*What about the prisoners, what should we do with them?*' He responded: '*You know what to do with them*!'[12]

'And the prisoners, what should we do with them?'
'The prisoners? You know what to do with them!' (*NARA*)

The Führer's instructions from Dietrich's staff also continued to flow down through the ranks. As they went down to the troops, they became clearer and clearer about the fate of the prisoners. At a staff meeting, Priess emphasised to the various Kampfgruppen leaders the need to *'fight with brutality and harshness without regard to the danger or consequences of the actions undertaken'*.[13] Thus, within SS-Sturmbannführer Knittel's units, which directly followed Kampfgruppe Peiper, the orders given were, among other things, that one must always advance, whatever the cost. The instructions further stated that if the situation required it, prisoners could be shot. It also emphasised that any armed or hostile civilians would be considered as partisans and had to be put to the sword.[14] However, Peiper states that he did not give any such instructions regarding the treatment of prisoners.[15]

As for the instructions given by Peiper, there has never been any irrefutable proof that he ordered the massacre of the GIs at Baugnez. In reality, the SS officer segmented his unit and ordered his officers to act independently in order to achieve the objectives set; his main objective being to progress with the greatest possible speed. He explained it as follows:

Although this photograph was taken at Baugnez, the massacre of eighty-four prisoners there was not the only one perpetrated by the 1. SS-Panzer-Division. (*NARA*)

> *Given the poor condition of the narrow roads, it would be impossible to change the marching order later, and therefore it was necessary to think about its composition and calculate it very carefully. That is why it took me two hours of reflection before discussing with my commanders. The march column under my command was 25 km long. Since radio communication was very limited because of the terrain, I chose a place in the centre of the column to occupy a key point. I therefore divided the column into several independent sections and made the command responsible for each one.*[16]

Thus, in the structure of the Kampfgruppe, each officer was at the head of his portion of the column. With this segmentation, it is difficult to determine the SS-Obersturmbannführer's real responsibilities. Nevertheless, in the sections under his command, the SS-Unterscharführer passed on a very direct order: '*no prisoners of war should*

Knittel told his Panzer-Grenadier that if the situation required it, then prisoners could be shot. (*NARA*)

The survivors described the events at the Dachau trial. (*NARA*)

be taken'.[17] SS officer Manfred Goblenz would affirm during his interrogation that the instructions he received before the battle specified that:

Peiper was one of the defendants at the trial. (*NARA*)

> *The armoured group, after a preliminary attack by a V.G. division (grenadiers of territorial troops) would have to push forward in enemy territory. This would provide the enemy with large open 'flanks'. The armoured group could therefore find itself in "distressing" situations and even be cut off from the rest of the army. Despite this, the mission was to penetrate forward without looking either to the left or to the right; this mission must be executed. In critically "tight" situations, prisoners of war could be shot.*[18]

At the Dachau trial, Knittel and Peiper were charged with different offences. Peiper was accused of having ordered not to take prisoners and of having ordered or authorised the shooting of prisoners and civilians. Meanwhile, Knittel was charged with having ordered prisoners and civilians to be shot. Both officers were considered morally and criminally responsible for the actions of their men. The prosecution's position was logical, because unarmed prisoners were killed and no special measures had been taken for the management of prisoners.

The Rules of War and the Germanic Interpretation

The ambiguity of the instructions given was not the only reason why the soldiers acted brutally. Since the beginning of 1944, specific measures had been taken to combat the Resistance, and these instructions were still in force at the time of the Ardennes offensive. Their existence contributed to multiplying the deleterious effect of the orders given in view of the offensive by providing a legal justification for the acts that were to be perpetrated.

Indeed, in order to pacify the rear zone of the armies and to eradicate the Maquis that were being formed in increasing numbers, Generalfeldmarschall Hugo Sperrle issued an order on 2 February 1944, the full text of which is given below:

> *Order concerning the fight against terrorists dated 2 February 1944.*
>
> 1. *Firearms must be used immediately. If innocent people are harmed, it is only the terrorists who are responsible for this unfortunate fact.*

Hugo Sperrle's (second from left) instructions had serious consequences for civilians, many of whom were victims of violence during the battle. (*NAC*)

2. *The location of the attack should be immediately identified and all civilians in the vicinity should be checked, regardless of person or rank.*
3. *The houses from which the shots were fired should be burnt down immediately. Report the facts to the command and security services only after these severe measures have been carried out.*
4. *The decision taken by the troop leader and the speed with which he acts are of primary importance. He must act brutally. If he does not, he will be severely punished for endangering the safety of the men under his command. To act with sluggishness or indecisiveness will be considered a dereliction of duty and respect due to the Reich Army.*
5. *Because of the current situation, no punitive measures that are too severe will be subject to sanction, except in the case of a breakdown in combat discipline.*

Signed, Sperrle[19]

This decision was clearly based on an interpretation of pre-1949 international humanitarian law, which stipulated, among other things, that civilians had a protected status and prohibited abuses against them, while also specifying that if maverick activity occurred, this legal protection fell away. Reprisals were then allowed in order to force the opponent to stop breaking the rules on his side. However, the coercive measures must remain proportional to the opponent's violations. This regulation was subject to a free

The battles on the Eastern Front contributed to the dehumanisation of the SS. (*NARA*)

assessment, which opened the door to actions that were considered illegal after the fact. The fact remains that high-ranking German soldiers, following the example of their Kaiserheer predecessors during the siege of Liège in August 1914, draped themselves in legality to justify punitive actions in Lidice or Oradour-sur-Glane.

The Influence of the Eastern Front

Several authors point to the fact that the merciless four-year conflict against the Bolshevik forces greatly influenced the progressive brutalization of the German army. In his book *Barbarossa and the Origins of the Final Solution*, Omer Bartov states unequivocally that: '*the war in the East created the preconditions for the Shoah, but also served to shape the mentality of the individual and to create a behaviour psychologically favourable to actions that would have been impossible to envisage in other circumstances.*'[20]

This undeniable psychological element would play an enormous role in the dramas that would take place in the Ardennes. To judge this, one only has to look at the report written for the American authorities on 7 April 1946 by Peiper himself. In it he describes with precision the particular atmosphere of the fighting in Russia and the adversary's mode of action. He underlined two characteristics of the Eastern Front. Firstly, he emphasised the contrast between western culture and the rusticity of the opponent: '*The German nerves were weakened by culture and civilisation. The superior weapon of a developed brain has worn itself out in the depths of the country. The efficiency of the human society of a cultured West has vanished against the primitive instinctive force of the fierce Asian onslaught.*' He then went on to describe the ferocity of the adversary he and his brothers in arms had to face: '*Two souls coexist in the body of a Russian soldier: the good, childlike nature of a simple man and the almost animal cruelty of the Asiatic.*' According to Peiper, the barbarity of the Red Army increased as it approached the borders of the Reich.

Peiper's Panzer-Grenadiers fought hard on the Russian steppes. Villages were attacked with no regard for civilians. This SS-Panzer-Grenadier unit is seen advancing through the snow, supported by a StuG III. (*NARA*)

These observations, made by an educated officer such as Joachim Peiper, were also made by others. Eventually, they lead to the feeling that the cultural superiority of the Aryan race was endangered by a less intelligent, but more ruthless opponent. For this culture to survive, there was no choice but to match the opponent in ferocity. These conceptions imported by the combatants on the Western Front contributed to creating a climate conducive to what took place in the Ardennes.

Secondly, Peiper clearly explained in the same report why the notion of the 'civilian' disappeared little by little from the minds of the units engaged against the Russians:

> *The Russians knew how to capitalise on the advantages offered by their own country. Civilians were forced to take part in the fighting, regardless of whether they were old men or women. Guns were widely available and their distribution continued. Talk about "civilians"! The pursuit battles of the winter of 1943–44 were like growing avalanches. After the recapture of a city like Kharkov, for example, the enemy captured 150,000 soldiers. The evacuation of a 30-km wide strip could never be put into practice. The German soldier who slept in a house one day knew that the next day he would find his host pursuing him on a T-34. The fighting became fiercer and fiercer and the concept of the civilian gradually disappeared.*[21]

This experience of combat in the east, combined with the testimonies gathered in the Ardennes, sheds light on the origin of the savagery of the acts committed on the banks of the Amblève.

As the fighting became increasingly fierce, the concept of the 'civilian' was gradually disappearing in the eyes of the SS. (*NARA*)

The Impact of the Belgian Resistance in September 1944

In the eyes of the SS soldiers, the Ardennes region had a very bad reputation. The Belgian War Crimes Commission's summary of the facts underlines that on arriving in the Stavelot region, SS elements were said to have declared: '*We know that the civilians here are at war with us. So we will wage war on the civilians.*'

Indeed, after the collapse of the Normandy front, the I. SS-Panzer-Korps, of which the 'Leibstandarte' was a part, withdrew through the Belgian Ardennes. In SS-Brigadenführer Fritz Kraemer's report describing the fighting of the survivors of the mechanised grouping, one section particularly stands out:

> *In general, the majority of the French population was not aggressive against the retreating troops, the situation was entirely different in Belgium … Very early on, the activities of the Belgian guerrillas caused us much anxiety. All over the Ardennes there were civilians shooting at German soldiers driving vehicles, walking individually or in small groups.*

The Belgian maquisards pressed the German troops hard during their retreat in the summer of 1944. (*NARA*)

> *It was impossible to send officers on special missions without security. Very often soldiers were found wounded, hidden in cellars by the resistance. Telephone lines were cut almost daily. Very frequently the roads were covered with iron traps that lacerated the tyres. This often slowed down movement. In contrast to the French guerrilla activities, the Belgian maquisards harassed the German troops with great insistence and inflicted many unnecessary losses.*[22]

Kurt Meyer's memoirs fully corroborate this view. During his withdrawal to the Meuse, he explained that the leaders of the III. and II. Abteilungen were lost in ambushes set up by partisans. In fact, the heavily wooded area through which they passed was conducive to the establishment of Maquis, who carried out destructive tasks during the Normandy campaign. Having been dormant from the second half of August onwards, they were put back on the alert on 1 September. The next day they were given the mission of informing the Allies about the movements in their sector and received parachuted weapons. On 3 September, as the 1. SS-Panzer-Korps, on the heels of the US VII Corps, began its movement through the Ardennes, the Secret Army, the main body of the Belgian resistance, received the order to go into action. The Maquis was set ablaze with the support of SAS groups, having been at work in eastern Belgium since 27 August. They were ordered to carry out harassment actions and set up ambushes on the routes taken by the retreating German troops. The missions were codenamed *Noah*, *Brutus*, *Bergbang* and *Caliban*.

Model understood the situation facing his troops very well. He made the right decisions and ordered a complete withdrawal behind the Westwall without delay. The I. SS-Panzer-Korps was given two routes: one in the north Namur–Aywaille–Malmedy-Bütgenbach Gap and the other in the south through Fumay–Libramont–Sûre–Vianden valley. The decision to retreat through the Ardennes was taken for very logical and tactical reasons. The wooded cover camouflaged their movements, which was even more important because the Germans did not have the control of the skies. The forest massif was the shortest route to the mother country and, finally, its wet cuts and steep relief made it an easy area to defend and perfect for an echeloned retreat. Paratroopers and maquisards collaborated efficiently, setting up ambush after ambush. On 4 September, as the American forces approached, small units of resistance fighters and maquisards were formed. Meanwhile, small units of resistance fighters and SAS multiplied the harassment actions on the German rear. The fighting resembled guerrilla actions.

Many officers of the 'Das Reich' division were lost in ambushes by partisans on the Ardennes roads. (*NARA*)

The retreat began on the night of 8/9 September, with three stopping positions taking advantage of the defensive virtues of the Ardennes valleys. The first line of resistance was on the Lesse, the second on the Ourthe and the Sûre, and the third on the Amblève and the Salm. For this manoeuvre, the 2. SS-Pz-Div was temporarily integrated into the I. SS-Panzer-Korps. The Allied air force did not cause much concern and the 2. SS-Pz-Div arrived safely at its destination on the night of 9/10 September. The remainder of the forces joined the following day. The 2. SS-Panzer-Division 'Das Reich' crossed the Westwall under cover of darkness the next

The heavily wooded area was conducive to the establishment of scrubland. (*NARA*)

day. To the great surprise of the Germans, the enemy did not pursue them! Kraemer states in his report: '*All the soldiers expected a breakthrough on the Rhine. They imagined a huge bombardment before the enemy troops. They did not even have to fight, the way was absolutely clear.*'

In addition, during the liberation of Belgium in September 1944, the 2. SS-Panzer-Division 'Das Reich' and the 'Hitlerjugend' suffered numerous ambushes and sabotage in the Amblève region. The SS saw this wooded area as a sanctuary for terrorist-infested Maquis. It should be remembered that SS-Sturmbannführer Waldmüller, one of the leaders of the two Kampfgruppe that escaped from the Falaise cauldron, lost his life in the nearby Lienne valley. No doubt the reports of these divisions returning to Germany fuelled the fear that the rear would be disorganised by the action of bands of maquisards. The bad reputation of the civilians in this region of the Ardennes may therefore also partly explain the behaviour of the SS troops when they returned three months later.

The following week, the stragglers crossed the wooded area. Alone or in small groups, fewer and fewer soldiers tried to reach their lines. All the while, the resistance continued its sweeping actions. It seemed that they did not always give the SS soldiers any trouble. Their reports kept in the archives of the Belgian army show disturbing statistics on this subject. A report by Major Bastin, commander of Zone V, states that: '*The following is a record of Germans killed in engagements with the SA or shot, after being found guilty of atrocities, from the arrival of American troops until 23/9/44 in S4 territory.*'[23]

Unit	Date	Officer	N/A Officer	Soldiers	Total	Location
S4	13/9	-	-	1 SS in civilian clothes	1	Werbomont
S4	18/9	-	-	1 SS	1	Mist (three bridges)
S4	15/9	-	-	2 SS	2	Bomal
S4	15/9	-	-	1 SS	1	?
S4	15/9	-	-	13 SS shot	13	Steinbach
S4	19/9	-	-	1 SS	1	Lierneux

The figures speak for themselves: nineteen SS prisoners were put to the sword. The document does not mention the holding of a trial to justify this decision.

The day before, the officer reported the capture of fourteen SS soldiers in Stavelot, where it appears that they were treated in accordance with the rules of war.

In his memoirs, Kurt Meyer states that he was mistreated by the Namur resistance. His testimony is interesting because it shows the unrest of the population against the captured soldiers and, in particular, the SS:

> *It was dark when we went through the door. Resistance fighters were watching the entrance. This was a bad sign. No sooner had the vehicles stopped than angry young men called out rudely and urged us to line up. The rifle butts rained down on the comrades who*

The Ardennes was seen as a rabbit warren where the resistance would have to be fiercely muzzled to prevent it from interfering in the combat zone. (*NARA*)

> *were the last to get out. I was on the right wing and I saw an American trying to parley with the resistance fighters and at the same time pointing at me. The resistance fighters nodded and invited me to follow them. They took me to the guardhouse where I was tied to a German warrant officer. While we were being tied, I heard the cries of pain from my comrades. The resistance fighters attacked a group of soldiers like savages. When I asked: "What is going on, what this for?" the adjutant answered: "They are shooting and killing all those in the SS and the paratroopers."As he said these last words, the first shots rang out in the courtyard. Thus, on 7 September 1944, about twenty German soldiers were criminally murdered in Namur. They did not die at the hands of Belgian soldiers, but under the bullets of excited kids, who wore their red scarves like medals.*[24]

Meyer forgets to mention that a few days earlier, his division had carried out reprisal actions against the villages on the heights of Dinant. The village of Sovet, for example, was the victim of a sweep reminiscent of the tragedy of Oradour. Thirteen people were killed, including the parish priest. There is no doubt that September 1944 in the Ardennes was the scene of a fight to the death between the SS and partisans. Back in their lines, the survivors would not forget the week of fighting in the Ardennes, where the resistance would have to be muzzled with ferocity to avoid it interfering in the combat zone.

Terror, that Extraordinary Weapon!

To these various influences must be added that of the SS system itself, which insisted that terror was a weapon to be used and taught as much to its recruits. In a speech given in April 1943, Himmler said to officers of the 1. SS-Panzer-Division: '*You who are in command, I ask you to constantly train the young people and to inculcate in them our world view. Terror is an extraordinary weapon.*'[25]

Himmler said to the officers of the 1. SS-Panzer-Division: '*You who are in command, I ask you to train the young people continuously and to instil in them our world view. Terror is an extraordinary weapon.*' (*NARA*)

In preparation for the offensive in the west, a new class of young recruits was incorporated into the ranks. Barely 16 or 17 years old, these inexperienced teenagers were supervised by veterans of the Eastern Front and were dropped into the turmoil of battle after less than three months' training. The 1. SS-Panzer-Division 'Leibstandarte SS Adolf Hitler' was no exception, with the particularity that its 'rookies' were supervised by a hardcore of veterans who had lived through the brutal experience of the Eastern Front. The Belgian War Crimes Commission also underlines the role played by the leadership:

> 'We *know from the participants in the killing themselves why these excesses were committed. Unterscharführer D…, commanding the platoon, furious that the group had been shot at as it passed through Stavelot, and making his men believe that civilians were the perpetrators, ordered the killing of all civilians encountered in the area. Private R… S…, soldier N…, states this categorically. He himself received direct but verbal orders from D… to do so with regard to all civilians. This order was carried out, but with the refinements of cruelty that we have seen. These soldiers made no secret of the brutality with which the murders were committed. The order was given by D… to the assembled platoon before reaching the hamlet of Parfondruy. During the roundup of which we have spoken, two young men, aged between 19 and 22, escorted by part of the incriminated platoon, escaped and ran towards a wood. Immediately Obersturmführer K… shouted: "Shoot, shoot, they must not escape". The soldiers fired: one of the civilians fell and was shot. And soldier T… added: "Those people hadn't shot at us. It was D… who ordered the killing of Parfondruy and Renardmont, and who had the idea of burning the corpses to death."*'[26]

The young recruits obeyed the ruthless orders of their elders, sometimes even surpassing them. (*NARA*)

Trial of a System

The interpretation of International Humanitarian Law in the form of instructions distributed to units could not lead to anything other than massacres of unarmed civilians. In the heat of battle, the line between an act of war and a crime is tenuous. Thus, by giving a licence to kill with relative autonomy, the OKW opened the door to the worst exactions without, however, provoking the same result through the different formations.

The wives of Peiper and Dietrich attended their husbands' trial in Dachau. (*NARA*)

The same orders given to the SS, indoctrinated in a system of 'values' specific to their corps, pushing back the psychological barriers of the human race, had tragic consequences on the populations of the occupied countries. While it is true that the distinction between the behaviour of Wehrmacht troops and Black Order [SS] units was no longer as clear-cut today as it was in the aftermath of the conflict, the fact remains that there were fewer abuses in the southern sector of the offensive, where traditional army formations were mainly involved. It is therefore possible to highlight the conjunctural influence of the formal instructions specific to all land formations and that of the Black Order doctrine. Together, these two superimposed systems could not logically produce anything other than repeated war crimes.

As for the killing of prisoners, Article 2 of the 1929 Geneva Convention protecting prisoners of war is more formal and does not leave room for interpretation. The orders given before the offensive in this regard were clear and unequivocal: no prisoners were to be taken. The decision to shoot prisoners may have been prompted by the need to advance into the enemy's position, without leaving enemy soldiers in the rear who could join their lines or organise resistance on the spot. It should be noted that this practice was not unique to the German army, and that similar excesses were observed in all camps in similar circumstances. There are many hypotheses as to the origin of the first shot that triggered the Baugnez massacre, and no one will ever be able to decide in favour of a particular thesis. Indeed, the American military justice system itself has not succeeded in doing so.

In fact, at the Dachau trial, which opened on 16 May 1945, Dietrich, Kraemer, Priess and Peiper were in the dock with sixty-nine companions belonging to the 1. SS-Panzer-Division. At the end of the trial two months later, forty-three death sentences were

At the end of the Dachau trial, forty-three death sentences were passed, including Peiper's. Few of the prisoners were actually executed. (*NARA*)

handed down, including that of Peiper. However, the defence lawyer, Colonel Willis Everett, succeeded in demonstrating that the interrogations and investigation were flawed, and the death sentences were consequently commuted to prison terms. Peiper was eventually released in 1956.[27]

It remains true, however, that because of the instructions distributed from echelon to echelon before the offensive was launched, and because of the absence of an appropriate structure for the evacuation of prisoners outside the zone of engagement, the German command had a significant share in the responsibility for the killings. Herein lies the complexity of deciding on the responsibility of the participants: which parts of their crimes should be attributed respectively to the system, the command, the circumstances and the combatants themselves? In any case, the system, without the will of those involved, could not have led to the murders.

Thus, in the context of the exactions committed by the SS in the Ardennes, several elements combine to produce tragedies. A framework that relied on terror as a weapon, the loss of the notion of differentiation between civilians and combatants justified by certain officers, the brutalisation of the conflict, a skilfully exploited legal vagueness, and deliberately ambiguous orders are all factors that make it possible to affirm that the criminal behaviour observed was the fruit of a context that was skilfully orchestrated by the will of the chain of command.

Chapter 8

From Ligneuville to the Heights of Stavelot

Helping Hands in Ligneuville

While the war crimes at Baugnez were taking place, the leading Panthers continued towards Ligneuville. Peiper says:

> *We had the information that there was a command post at Ligneuville, but we arrived too late, we only got their lunch! This happened between 11:00 and 13:00 on 17 December. Nevertheless, we encountered strong resistance on the way out of the town. We encountered American tanks for the first time and lost a Panther and two other armoured vehicles.*

The locality was occupied by the train elements of Combat Command B of the 9th Armored Division. It was in this location that Peiper claims to have had his first

As the leading Panthers continued towards Ligneuville, one of them was lost in front of the Hôtel des Ardennes. (*NARA*)

Concern about the breakthrough spread among the American ranks. (*NARA*)

encounter with American armour.[1] The maintenance section of the 14th Tank Battalion was about to join the main body of the formation deployed in the St. Vith sector. The mechanics were working on two broken down tanks: a Sherman M4 105mm fire support tank and a Sherman Tank Dozer. The Americans were warned that the Germans were coming by soldiers running down from Baugnez. General Timberlake, who commanded the 49th Anti-Aircraft Brigade, was in the locality with his staff. It was 14:00 and the American officer had just finished dinner with his deputies at the Hôtel du Moulin. He only had time to run away. Peiper knew that there was a command post in the village and ordered his Panzerspitze,[2] consisting of two Panthers and a half-track, to rush to capture and secure the bridge over the Amblève. The idea was simple, but it worked: drive full throttle through the city, take advantage of the element of surprise, capture the bridge and secure it. SS-Obersturmführer[3] Werner Sternebeck[4] was in charge of the operation:

> *We entered Ligneuville and advanced to the bridge over the Amblève. On the orders of the Kampfgruppe, the leading armoured elements had to stop and secure the bridge. The Panzer-Pioniere searched under the bridge for explosive charges. They were wounded by machine gun fire. As soon as the stretcher-bearers arrived to take away the wounded, the automatic weapons fell silent. Opposite the church there was a large hotel.*[5] *The caretaker of the hotel seemed to be waiting for us. I gave the order to stop and asked about the enemy soldiers. I was so surprised by his answer that I can still repeat it today: "Good morning, sir. The general left with his staff a few minutes ago, but he will be back by Christmas". Surprised by this information, I left my Panzer and went into the hotel to find that the dinner table had not yet been cleared. Lit cigarettes and still half-filled glasses confirmed to me the sudden evacuation of the headquarters.*[6]

Very quickly, other German tanks entered the town to reinforce the leading elements. It should be noted that at this time only the bridge was secured, and that Americans were still present in the area. Arndt Fischer and his Panther No. 152 burst onto the road leading down from the ridges. The machine was destroyed a few metres from the Hôtel du Moulin. The German officer recounted his misadventure:

> *We knew that the* Spitze *was very weak, with its two tanks and a few half-tracks. As we had no other tanks immediately available, my Panther and behind me SS-Standartenführer Joachim Peiper's half-track followed the leading elements as fast as we could. To begin with, I did not notice any fighting and therefore wanted to cross the bridge. At the curve before the bridge I was hit from behind. My Panther burst into flames. We evacuated the machine under machine gun and rifle fire from the nearby houses. We were burning like torches, as only two hours earlier we had refuelled and filled our cans at Büllingen. In doing so we had soaked our clothes with fuel. My driver never made it out and died completely burnt in the box. I think Peiper covered me with his fire and protected us from the fire from the houses.*[7]

Fischer's tank was hit by one of the Shermans of the 14th Tank Battalion left in the village to be repaired. The mechanics were surprised by the arrival of the first wave and fired at the tank of the second wave. They let the tank pass and destroyed it from behind, where its armour was thinner. The Sherman was destroyed by Peiper himself using a Panzerfaust.

Alfons Sproß belonged to the SS-Aufklärungs-Abteilung 1[8] and was following in the column, his mission being to capture the US command post:

> *In Blankenheim we had received a new American armoured reconnaissance car, a Greyhound,*[9] *but as it was a captured vehicle that should have been used in the framework of the Greif operation*[10] *and was not working, we had to repair it. We were finally very happy to climb in it. When we were driving it, I had noticed that when we were climbing up steep streets it was not as powerful as our own Pumas and we thought that was because the German petrol had a lower octane rating than the Americans had. We were ordered to go as fast as possible to Ligneuville as there was still the possibility of capturing a US command post. When we arrived at the café we saw American soldiers who had moved to the right side of the road.*[11]

The testimonies of the three German fighters agree that the American defence was fierce. The maintenance platoon of the 14th Tank Battalion managed to extract itself from the town almost completely, losing only the men trapped on the wrong side of the River Amblève, who later surrendered to the SS after a brave fight. Eight prisoners were selected and lined up along the road by a ditch, where they were shot in cold blood in the back of the head.[12] The rest, on the other side of the river, held their positions until 16:00 before withdrawing in good order. It was winter and night was already falling at the end of the day on 17 December. The Gepanzerte Kampfgruppe was still far from its objective, and needed to seize another bridge over the Amblève at Stavelot. The meandering river marked the route of the German force, which would have to cross it many times.

The Fallschirmjäger were carried into the column. (*NARA*)

After regrouping, the Kamfgruppe took to the road again towards Stavelot via small roads, crossing the hamlets of Pont, Refat, and Beaumont without any problem. Shortly after nightfall, the first elements arrived at Lodomez, 3 kilometres from the small town of Stavelot, where the bridge, one of the few in the region, had to ensure the passage of heavy Panzers. The capture of this work of art, which dates from the Middle Ages, was essential because the Amblève, a torrential river with steep banks and surrounded by forests, formed an impassable anti-tank barrier for vehicles.

A Handful of Engineers against a Panzer

Although the German breakthrough was well behind its initial schedule, the speed of its progress exceeded the American capacity to react. Surprise was still in the Germans' favour, but not for much longer as the first American reinforcements were already being sent to block their path. After the capture of Ligneuville, however, there was still virtually nothing in the path of Peiper's Panzer.

Although the attack in the sector had indeed surprised the Americans by its scale, they were not slow to react. The method of combat put in place on the whole front was the same: to gain time. Behind the screen of energetically defending troops, a stop position was set up to delay the attacker, while the US command carefully chose the place where it would receive the next shock and deployed its troops there. On the route of the Gepanzerte Kampfgruppe, Stavelot was chosen to play this role. From a tactical point of view, this was a good option. With only one bridge across the river Amblève, behind it the old medieval town, with its buildings and narrow streets, was ideal to resist an armoured assault. To reach the town, the German tanks had to take the corniche: a hillside road where they would present their more vulnerable flanks under fire from anti-tank guns before reaching the bridge.

The only troops available to try to slow down the German advance were elements of the American combat engineers, in particular the 1111th Engineer Combat Group,

Only the US engineer units were left to slow Peiper down. (*NARA*)

a formation commanded by Colonel Wallis Anderson. Created in 1943, this type of structure was more flexible than the combat engineer regiments, and was used centrally at corps and army level. The headquarters of a combat engineer group commanded three to four battalions reinforced by the resources of a light equipment company, a dump truck company and a maintenance company. Although some engineer regiments still existed in the forward section communication area, the group represented the largest army-level combat engineer organisation. Normally, five combat engineer groups support each army. Usually one or more engineer battle groups support each corps.

Unfortunately for them, on 16 December 1944 the 1111th Engineer Combat Group (ECG) occupied positions directly on the axis of advance of the 5. and 6. Panzer-Armeen. The engineer formation was anchored in a 60-kilometre arc, with its companies scattered over an area of 250 km^2 between Dinant on the Meuse and Eupen, just south of Aachen. The 291st Engineer Combat Battalion (ECB) was stationed at Basse-Bodeux, while the

Engineers used their skills to build roadblocks by blasting down trees. (*NARA*)

51st ECB was more than 20 kilometres south-west at Marche, and the 296th ECB was at Sourbrodt (near Eupen). The 629th Light Equipment Company was located east of Bütgenbach. If we look more precisely at the units located near Peiper's next assault, they included B Company of the 291st ECB; the 962nd Engineer Maintenance Company in Malmedy; C Company of the 202nd ECB in Stavelot and the Group Headquarters with elements of the 291st ECB in Trois-Ponts, right on the route to be taken by the 1. SS-Panzer-Division.

The usual tasks assigned to the 1111th ECG were not strictly speaking combat missions. Colonel Anderson was responsible for engineering work in the area, providing close support to V Corps and security missions in the rear lines. In addition to normal activities such as bridge repair, road maintenance, snow removal, and forestry and quarrying, the 1111st ECG was heavily involved in the operation of forty-one sawmills to produce lumber for bridge construction and winter quarters. Although they were technical specialist troops, they were tactically expected to be able to intervene to support the infantry in the front line. In the US Army, this practice had existed since the First World War, when it was necessary to help infantrymen break through barbed wire and destroy fortified strongpoints.[13] While American engineers did not have the firepower of infantry, they were particularly adept at erecting obstacles to aid the progress of armoured units using mines, fallen tree trunks etc.

Stopping Peiper with Nothing!

It was at 02:00 on the night of 16/17 December that the First US Army issued a general alert report indicating that paratroop drops had taken place and that a large-scale enemy counter-attack was possible. At 10:00, the leader of the 1111th ECG, Colonel Wallis Anderson, was informed that his 629th Light Equipment Company had been attacked by an armoured combat group. Colonel Anderson immediately understood the seriousness of the situation and proceeded to do a quick assessment of the disposition of his group, which was practically alone in front of the German armoured tide that was breaking through the Ardennes. The 291st Engineer Combat Battalion of Lieutenant Colonel David E. Pergrin was given the task by Anderson to prepare the destruction of the bridges in the region and to block the different accesses leading to Malmedy. Furthermore, Pergrin was ordered to take charge of all the units of the group present in the Malmedy area, to inform himself of the situation and to take the necessary measures to prevent the German advance.

As part of this training, 3rd Squadron, 2nd Platoon, C Company of the 291st ECB was ordered to take over the Stavelot Bridge. Sergeant Chuck Hensel commanded the twelve men sent to Stavelot to establish a barricade. He loaded his truck with explosives, firing cords, mines, a bazooka and a machine gun. Arriving at the location at 18:30, the sergeant was surprised by the amount of traffic with all its lights on. He was ordered to set up a

Small squads were dispatched in all directions. (*NARA*)

roadblock on the ledge at the top of the Chemin du Château. The non-commissioned officer was experienced, but did not yet know that a powerful German armoured column was heading towards him. In 1982, he explained in detail what happened that evening:

> *Just before the top of the hill, the street turned right. After the bend it became less steep and even flat on the plateau. On the way up, I probed the terrain for an ideal spot. But our driver couldn't turn around on the narrow road and we had to continue upwards to find a place to turn around. Then we slowly descended. At the bend, which was now on our left, I ordered the driver to stop. I was convinced that this was the ideal place to build the barricade. The rock on our left hid the view of the road. The gorge on the right was about 20 metres deep. Some of my men built a wooden barrier while the others laid thirteen mines from one side of the road to the other, so that a vehicle passing through the bend in the road would not see them until they were on top of them. I ordered Bernard Goldstein to stand guard behind the bend. Corporal Eugene Morris accompanied him to a small shed. Neither of them knew that at the same moment, not far from them, the men of the first Peiper tanks were wondering whether or not to cross the Stavelot bridge.*
>
> *When Morris returned, I ordered him and Gadzolia to hold his position with a bazooka. Thirty metres back, Leary and Lynch took up a position behind our machine gun. It was now 19.30. I was worried because Goldstein was alone on sentry duty. His best friend, Bauers, agreed to join him. As he did not know exactly where Goldstein was, I accompanied him to the bend. In the meantime, three German tanks tried to approach with infantry. Goldstein was worried about being behind the shed as he only had an M1 rifle. He heard the tanks approaching. They moved very slowly and silently through the night so that Goldstein, who could speak German, could hear a few words spoken by the infantry.*
>
> *At this moment Charlie Bauers and I reached the rock in the bend, not far from Goldstein's post. Then we heard the engines of the tanks a hundred yards from the shed behind which Goldstein had hidden, and we stopped, transfixed. We couldn't believe our ears when Goldstein shouted in a loud voice: "Halt!" It was funny, crazy and unreal. Imagine Goldstein, with a rifle as his only weapon, ordering the German behemoths to stop! When they heard Goldstein's voice, the German infantrymen jumped out of their tanks and opened fire. Bauers and I also fired. But when the machine gun opened fire, we quickly retreated behind the rocks. The Germans then started firing with their 75-mm gun. Morris and Gadzolia responded with their bazooka. For Leary and Lynch, it was senseless to fire the machine gun. They couldn't see the enemy and the tanks were not moving very fast. Some of us thought it would be better to withdraw to the bridge. Our barricade was finished anyway. The German tanks would jump on our mines if they dared to advance. But what happened to Goldstein? He didn't come with us and we were afraid that he was wounded. The men didn't want to abandon their comrade.*
>
> *After a few minutes, the German fire stopped. Bauers then tried to leave his shelter behind the rock to find Goldstein. He was immediately greeted by a burst of machine gun fire and quickly retreated. For a few minutes we didn't know what to do. Again, we*

heard the engines of the tanks and the clatter of the tracks. The Germans were gradually withdrawing. Gadzolia, in his turn, suggested going to look for Goldstein. He walked towards the bend and saw a tank. It was leaning a bit as if it had slipped. Gadzolia came back and told us what he had seen. I decided that it was time to go back to the bridge. We loaded the bazooka and the machine gun and let our truck roll downhill. We started the engine when we are almost at the bottom.[14]

The Impact of a Scuffle

The incident above was not the main reason for the temporary halt of KG Peiper, but it was a major factor. By 16:00 on 17 December, the reconnaissance elements had already reached the heights of the town and reported back. The view from this high vantage point allowed them to discover a huge traffic jam: the columns of the 7th Armored Division on their way to St. Vith. The traffic made Peiper think that Stavelot was heavily defended and in the eyes of the SS officer, the town seemed to be completely jammed with several hundred trucks. In the early evening he said he had tried to capture Stavelot, but the terrain was too difficult so he gave up. In September 1945 he would say:

As KG Peiper was brought to a halt, this tanker is waiting for instructions before continuing its progression. (*NARA*)

At 16:00 on 17 December 1944 we reached the Stavelot area, which was heavily defended. We could see heavy traffic on the way to Malmedy through Stavelot, and Stavelot itself seemed to be completely jammed with several hundred trucks. That night the terrain presented great difficulties. The only possible approach was from the main road and the terrain to the left of the road descended very steeply and to the right of the road it climbed in the same way. There was a short curve at the entrance to Stavelot, on which several Shermans and anti-tank guns were pointed. Thereupon we pounded Stavelot with heavy infantry howitzers and mortars, causing great confusion in the town and the destruction of several depots. At the same time I ordered one of my Panzer IV companies to try to find a way around Stavelot through Aisomont, Warne and Trois-Ponts. It took a small path which was almost impossible to negotiate with the tanks. At 18:00 a counter-attack went round a high hill 800 metres east of Stavelot and hit my column from the south.[15]

The halting of the advance allowed the troops to rest. (*NARA*)

In reality, Peiper was not on the heights of Stavelot that evening. Instead, he was in Ligneuville, where he spent part of the night. The leading edge of the attack was under the orders of SS-Sturmbannführer Werner Poetschke, the commander of the Panther Abteilung.[16] This is why his account of the facts exaggerates the magnitude of the American reaction. On learning of the stoppage, he ordered his Panzer IVs, which were lighter than the Panthers, to find a way around the town via Aisomont, Wanne and Trois-Ponts. If Stavelot presented him with a few complications, they were nothing compared to Trois-Ponts, a city which, as its name indicates, has three river branches to cross. By passing through Wanne, he could hope to take the bridge over the Amblève in reverse. Peiper later explained: '*I had a Panzer-Grenadiere Abteilung in my column. When darkness fell we observed heavy American road traffic to the west, with no blackout measures applied. We fired on it at a distance of 4,500 metres with our tanks, but did not mount a further counter-attack until dawn on 18 December. I assigned another armoured infantry Kompanie against the town.*'[17] This infantry company was part of the regiment of SS-Sturmbannführer Josef Diefenthal. Diefenthal began by securing the approaches to the city with his Panzergrenadiere Abteilung. His SS took position at 04:00 on the left bank in the houses overlooking Stavelot.

As for the difficulties of the terrain, it must be stressed that the embryonic ambush on the heights corresponds to a place where it was difficult to manoeuvre with tanks. Sergeant Hensel's truck (291st Engineer Combat Battalion) was unable to turn around. K. Wortmann, who served in the anti-aircraft company 10. (Flak)/SS-Pz-Rgt 1 described the situation from the troops' point of view:

The mobile artillery followed Peiper. (*NARA*)

Early in the afternoon we reached Ligneuville. We stayed there for a short time. Our tanks were parked in front of the bridge over the Amblève. We stayed near our engines. At dusk, we received the order to continue. Because of the strong enemy resistance, we could not follow our route (which passed through Recht), we agreed to continue in the direction of Stavelot through the valley of the Amblève. The road was very narrow and winding with some small villages. We moved slowly. Moreover, we did not know the position and strength of the enemy. But we did not meet any Americans until we reached Stavelot. There were only delays due to difficult bends and large rocks on the left side of the road. Our Panther tanks had to take several turns to negotiate the curves. The first of them broke its gun on rocks.[18] *We stayed on this narrow road to Stavelot throughout the night of 17/18 December. We could not sleep because of the cold. Several comrades visited the few small farms and we made some tea and coffee.*[19]

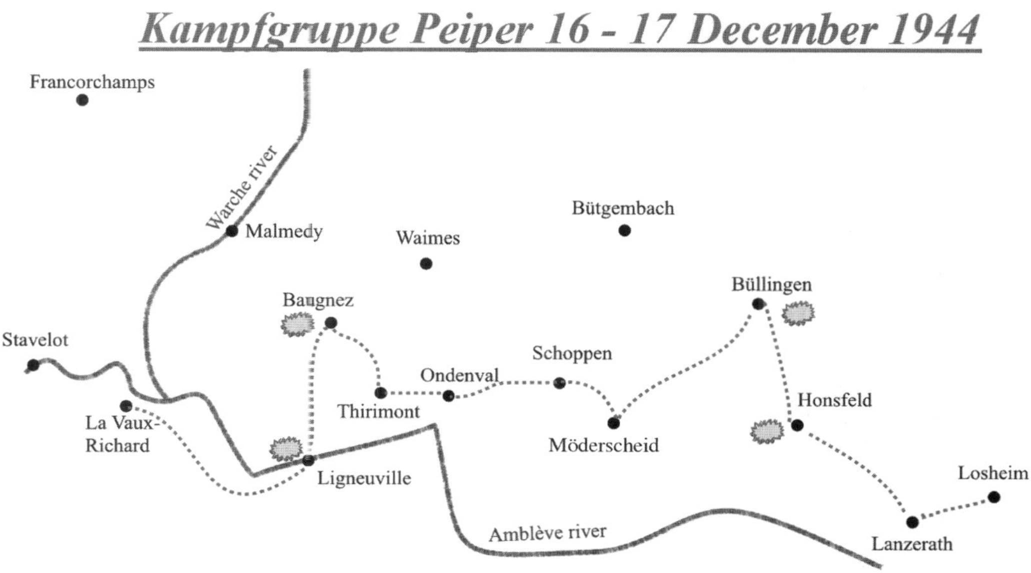

The route of the Peiper column after two days of battle. (*Coll. Authors*)

At the time Peiper made his decision, the town of St Remacle was largely undefended. Indeed, the appearance of the US engineer squad on the Chemin du Château probably suggested that winning the battle at night, with insufficient infantry, was going to be a difficult task. It should not be forgotten, however, that its troops had been fighting non-stop since 16 December. The men had been in action for over forty-eight hours and were exhausted. The columns were disorganised, the artillery that should have supported an attack was still far behind. Everything was in place to push the German colonel to stop and regroup his forces and reorganise them for the double assault on Stavelot and Trois-Ponts. This decision, although partly logical, was to have serious repercussions for what followed. If he had decided to attack at that moment, nothing could have stopped Peiper and his irruption on the artery linking Malmedy to Trois-Ponts would have generated great difficulties for the American forces, and in particular for the logistic tail of the 7th Armored Division, whose mission was to defend the strategic road junction of St. Vith. Moreover, the US command quickly recovered from the surprise it had suffered on 16 December and took advantage of the opportunity to continually reinforce the town's garrison.

The 30th ID was ordered to move towards Stavelot. (*NARA*)

A Sheman battalion accompan_ed the GIs charged with retaking Stavelot. (*NARA*)

Chapter 9

Kampfgruppe Peiper Breaks Through in Stavelot

Armoured Infantry to the Rescue

Although Sergeant Hensel's squad had averted the disaster, the situation in Stavelot was not yet stable. The 526th Armored Infantry Battalion (AIB) and its adjoining A Company of the 825th Tank Destroyer Battalion were urgently sent to the area to fill the gaps in the position until the arrival of the 30th Infantry Division 'Old Hickory'. The two small formations reached the edge of Malmedy at about 02:00 on 18 December. Fearing for its communications, the 12th Army Group ordered a company and a platoon of anti-tank vehicles to be sent to Stavelot. Consequently, A Company of the 526th AIB and 1st Platoon of A Company, 825th TD Battalion, equipped with 3-inch towed guns, were dispatched to Stavelot at about 03:00. These precautions were logical as the town was a key position for three reasons: there was an excellent bridge over the Amblève, there were two important roads in the network that led to Liège, and the town was only 15 kilometres from Spa, where the headquarters of the First US Army was located.

The anti-tank guns of the 825th TD Battalion did not have the opportunity to take up a position and had to retreat to the other side of the river. (*NARA*)

On arriving at the scene, what seemed necessary to be carried out immediately was to send reinforcements to the ledge to maintain Sergeant Hensel's roadblock. Two platoons were given the mission to cross the Amblève bridge accompanied by two 3-inch towed guns. These reinforcements set off at about 05:00, but had barely had time to climb a section of the sloping road leaving Stavelot when they came under fire from SS-Panzergrenadieren supported by tanks. The anti-tank guns did not have the opportunity to take up position and the reinforcements were forced to retreat to the other side of the river. The after action report of the tank destroyer gives details of what happened:

The first platoon arrived in Stavelot at approximately 03:30 on 18 December 1944. Major Solis, the commander of the forces there, sent one platoon from Company A of the 526th AIB and a section of the first platoon across the river to occupy the positions on the heights of the town. The first platoon crossed the river at approximately 05:45 and was in contact with the enemy at about 06:05 hours. This section was unable to reach the designated positions because of enemy fire and in attempting to withdraw to meet the enemy's fire, both guns and their half-tracks were destroyed. As a result of this action, six men were missing and two were wounded. At dawn, the enemy shelled the town of Stavelot. The fire came from machine guns and heavy weapons in the houses overlooking the town.[1]

The infantrymen of the 526th AIB also withdrew in disorder. Engaged on the open bridge, they lost a third of their strength. In fact, it seems that the Americans had fallen into a trap cleverly set by the 11. Kompanie of the SS-Panzergrenadier-Regiment 2, having let the column approach right under their windows before firing. Unfortunately, the open structures of the American half-tracks made easy targets for grenades when thrown from the first floor of a house.

The Panzergrenadiere tried to take advantage of the disarray caused by the trapped GIs rushing back by pursuing them across the bridge in force. SS-Scharführer Rayer recalled:

The 11. Kompanie was ordered to take the bridge. [...] Only the 1. and 2. Zuge were available. Thus, due to a mechanical problem, the rest of the Kompanie was far behind. Only the Wilfer section of my Zug was available. The bridge was taken, but could not be held. The Kompanie established itself on one side of the bridge and was in a very difficult position. The enemy tanks kept moving and we could do nothing about it. We suffered considerable losses. [...] On Diefenthal's orders, I took command of the Kompanie. At the first light of dawn, the Panzers came to us. As soon as they arrived, we continued.[2]

The Irresistible Panther Charge

Peiper prepared his assault on the town:

> *I pulled two Panthers 200 metres from the town limits and ordered them to charge at full speed. They drove around the short curve at the entrance to the town, firing rapidly. The first Panther was hit and burned, but had enough momentum to penetrate the anti-tank obstacle at the turn and damage two Shermans. The second vehicle used this opportunity to get through and seize the bridge. We followed with other vehicles and the Americans evacuated the town, abandoning their equipment.*[3]

The SS-Standartenführer's testimony is, at the very least, questionable. At the time of the assault, there were no Shermans in the town and, as we shall see, the Panther that was hit was not the one that led the attack.

The first Panther to set off was SS-Obersturmführer Zimmerman, who was thus the first to cross the bridge over the Amblève. He explained how he charged at full speed:

> *Peiper himself chose my tank to lead the attack through Stavelot, which was to take place at first light. The whole crew was given clear instructions: "Just beyond the curve there is an anti-tank gun,*[4] *you had better go into fifth gear. There is an officer of ours lying in the middle of the bridge. We don't know if he is dead or wounded. Take care of that officer."*

Panther 115 was not the one leading the attack. (*NARA*)

Panther 111 took part in the Stavelot attack and fell on the bridge. (*NARA*)

> *Slowly, it was getting light. We started our engines to warm them up. "Fahrer Vorwärts!"*[5] *We met no resistance. The anti-tank was there but we pushed it out of the way. On the bridge! No officers. As soon as we were on the bridge we were hit. "Richtschütze Feuer!"*[6] *The 75mm fired, but we did not hit our target. Our barrel was pointing to the sky after the hit. "Fahrer beschleunigt!"*[7] *We rolled on the anti-tank gun's crutch. It broke and ended up on the driver's hatch. There was shooting from all sides, but it gradually diminished. We had broken through!*[8]

The anti-tank gun referred here to is probably Sergeant Smith's 57-mm gun M1. The American infantry was then only equipped with 57mm tubes derived from the British Ordnance Quick-Firing 6-pounder. Lacking power, these were unable to disable a Panther from the front, so the gun leader moved his gun to an alley perpendicular to the bridge exit. He was thus protected from fire coming from the opposite bank and could possibly have had an opportunity to pierce the armour of the German tank by a flanking shot.[9] Captain Ferris described the scene from the US side:

> *The anti-tank platoon leader was killed at his piece. One gun was forced to cease firing and another was driven back. The third gun, manned by Sergeant Elvan Smith and*

> *Private Taylor, continued to fire until the lead tank came within 35 yards of its location. By this time all available ammunition in the vicinity had been fired and the gun crew was forced to abandon the tube.*[10]

The assault ordered by Peiper was well coordinated. The Panthers attacked in column while supporting fire accompanied the progression of the tanks, closely followed by the Panzergrenadiere. The infantrymen of the 526th AIB did not give up easily. Sergeant Major Boyd Williams and a bazooka team went upstairs to a house with windows looking directly onto the bridge. The only chance to stop a Panther was to break the track with a well-aimed shot. The GIs succeeded in doing this on the tank that followed Zimmerman's, Panther No. 111, and the Panzer was immobilised on the bridge. The bridge was not as wide as it is today, however, and the Panther blocked the entire deck. Zimmerman was isolated from his brothers in arms on the other side. No. 113 was at the bottom of the street and received an order from the company commander, SS-Obersturmführer Kremser, to help. The officer organised covering fire to allow the operation to take place. Exposing himself, Kremser was wounded in the stomach and

Panther 115 was the only one to be destroyed during the attack (*Jacobs Collection Stavelot Library*)

had to be evacuated. A rope was finally attached to No. 111 and it was removed so that progress could continue.[12] However, this halt caused a collateral victim. In fact, the tank that Peiper mentions in his testimony was No. 115. Arriving in the middle of the Rue du Vieux Château, it was obliged to stop to wait for the situation to clear at the bridge. The stop would prove fatal, as the machine found itself in the line of fire of one of the two remaining anti-tank guns of the 825th TD Battalion. This one, under the command of Sergeant Hauser, was installed in the city on the Avenue Jean Nicolay and was pointing south. The distance was approximately 400 metres and the power of the 3-inch gun was sufficient to pierce the Panther's side. It hit the engine compartment, causing the tank to burst into flames, as the crew evacuated.

The Crossing of Stavelot

The second line of resistance consisted of the two surviving 3-inch guns belonging to Hauser and Celentano, which were located on the Malmedy road in the centre of town, above the abbey's meadow. Lieutenant Doherty, who commanded them, reorganised his position, placing Hauser's gun in such a way as to flank the Panzers coming up through the town, and Celentano's gun in such a way as to engage the enemy coming up the cornice. The presence of the US guns forced the SS to choose another route through the town. They did not take the Rue du Châtelet, but the Rue du Haut Rivage, so as not to be in the line of fire of the anti-tanks. A duel ensued and fifteen shots were fired from Hauser's gun, the exchange of fire blocking the German advance. Around 10:00, the evacuation order was given to the US troops.

The after action report of the 825th TD Battalion then becomes clearly erroneous, particularly regarding the destruction of a Tiger tank which would not enter Stavelot until well after the unit had evacuated the town. Unfortunately, the report can no longer be taken into account when reconstructing the facts. In reality, it seems that from this moment on, the resistance completely collapsed and all the survivors evacuated the town by sabotaging Hauser's gun with a thermal grenade.

A boulevard was now clear for Peiper's Panzer, which rushed at full speed towards Trois-Ponts. The Americans withdrew from the town via two separate routes, one towards Francorchamps via the Rue de la Haute Levée, the other towards Malmedy. During their retreat north, the GIs passed by a huge fuel depot. Peiper, however, thought only of taking advantage of his easy breakthrough in Stavelot to seize the bridges of Trois-Ponts by surprise. He then made the mistake of not masking the approaches to the town with an infantry detachment. This was an unnecessary precautionary measure, as he thought he was being closely followed by Kampfgruppe Knittel and wanted to keep his full strength to face the next obstacle.

Knittel's reinforcements were still a long way behind, however, and were now passing Kaiserbaracke. Knittel, fearing Stavelot would be occupied in force, reorganised his column and made the 2. Kompanie of SS-Obersturmführer Manfred Coblenz's SS-Aufklärungs-Abteilung 1 take the lead because it was equipped with armoured semi-trailers mounted by veterans. It was therefore the most capable of taking the city. Coblenz explained in a statement:

KG Knittel was rerouted from Kaiserbaracke to support Peiper. (*NARA*)

> *At Kaiserbaracke, Knittel informed me that the main part of the column would follow Kampfgruppe Hansen and continue its way to Recht. He instructed my company to secure the crossroads and ordered me to personally conduct an offensive reconnaissance towards Saint-Vith in order to locate the enemy. Immediately, I ordered my second in command, SS-Ustuf. Siebert, to disembark the men and set up a defensive perimeter in the woods around the crossroads. As for me, with three other SPWs,*[12] *I turned left and advanced for several kilometres towards Saint-Vith, without encountering the slightest sign of any enemy presence. It was then that I decided to stop the vehicles and to scout on foot, accompanied by some men. I had barely gone a few hundred metres when the sound of an approaching motorbike made me turn back. Back at the SPW, the motorcyclist – a liaison officer sent by Knittel – informed me that I had to return to Kaiserbaracke. Once back at the crossroads, SS-Ustuf. Siebert handed me a sheet of paper on which Knittel had scribbled his orders. There was no question of following Hansen via Recht, we had to go back north and join the group in Stavelot. Knittel even said that once there, I would take the lead and force my way through the town before linking up with Kampfgruppe Peiper, somewhere beyond Trois-Ponts. So we put the engines of our SPWs back in gear and left the crossroads. As we left, I looked at my watch; it was just 13:00.*[13]

The time provided by Coblenz is German time, one hour ahead of American time. It was almost two hours since the first Peiper vehicles had passed through Stavelot without masking their flanks. The Americans did not stand still…

The Fuel Depot

The fuel depot that KG Peiper came close to was guarded by Belgian soldiers. The Haute Levée depot had been guarded by a dozen men of the 5th Rifle Battalion, under the orders of Lieutenant Detroz, since 14 December. At daybreak, the officer arrived at a property called La Bicoque, a charming half-timbered Ardennes house. The men disembarked from the GMC, including sergeants Arpigny, Albert Vermeulen and Marcel Magain,[14]

Belgian riflemen defended the bridge of the Haute Levée. (*Museum of Ardennes Hunters*)

followed by Corporal Pierre Suinen.[15] The riflemen were Robert Tille, Robert Lemaire, Paul Wantier, Jean Ingels, Elomir Cambier, Jean Lesire and Alfred Cantigneau. The depot began about 100 metres in front of La Bicoque, towards Stavelot, and extended for about 1 kilometre towards the village of Francorchamps. Poorly armed with Lee Enfield rifles and a Bren,[16] the men were on the alert, but took their places in front of the pile of jerry cans. Such a reserve of petrol could never be allowed to fall into the hands of the enemy.

Early in the morning, when the fighting in Stavelot began, the removal of the fuel reserves on the road to the Francorchamps circuit and in Bista started. It was completed before noon. The removal was done by trucks of the 3814th QM Gas Supply 1st Army. Pfc Theo Lauter was part of this transport unit and recalled that:

We were operating the huge fuel depot that was scattered in the woods between Spa and Stavelot, about 5 million gallons of petrol, diesel and lubricants. On the morning of 18 December 1944 we were awakened by the sound of explosions. We were supposed to be well behind the lines so we were not too worried. Someone said he thought it was pioneers blowing up fortifications so that the Germans could not use them again in case of a counter-attack. But this was not the case as the explosions were getting closer and closer. Finally, our sergeant arrived on the scene with orders to pack up and get out of there, as the Germans were in Stavelot on the other side of the Amblève. The explosions we heard were German artillery. We did not need to be told twice to evacuate. We went back to Spa and later that evening some of us went back to the fuel dump near Stavelot where the evacuation of fuel was being carried out.

Large fuel deposits were scattered along Peiper's route. (*NARA*)

> *Our job was to direct the trucks as they were taken to various locations further behind the lines. If I remember correctly, there were trucks from just about every unit in the First Army and most of the fuel was safely evacuated. We were on duty there all night and we could hear the German tanks at Stavelot. By this time units of the 30th Division, the 82nd Airborne Division and the 3rd Armored Division had arrived and had prevented the Germans from crossing the Amblève. I think if the Germans had captured the fuel depot it would certainly have changed the course of history.*[17]

A stream of GIs and vehicles started to pass in front of the Belgian soldiers. The Americans withdrew towards Francorchamps. Major Solis, commander of the infantrymen of the 526th AIB, ordered the withdrawal of his troops; some went astray via the road to Malmedy, while the majority of the survivors entered the Haute Levée. At the back, a command car arrived containing Major Solis. He ordered his driver to stop at Lieutenant Detroz and explained the situation to the Belgian officer: the fuel must not fall into enemy hands. As the last American vehicles passed, Detroz decided to set fire to the three piles of jerry cans in front of La Bicoque. There was a great deal of confusion among the troops, who had never been taught to set fire to a fuel depot. Someone suggested firing at the Bren with incendiary cartridges, so Robert Tille, who was in charge of the Bren, walked away and fired into the pile of jerry cans. Nothing happened. In fact, for reasons of stealth, the tracer bullets only took effect after about 50 metres and so were unable to set fire to the fuel. The only option left was the classic one: spreading the fuel and setting it on fire.[18] Henry Stairs, a technician (T/5) in the 1st Battalion HQ Company, 117th Infantry Regiment, recalled:

> *An attempt by the Germans to take over the petrol depot seemed imminent. The order to burn the depot was given to the 5^{e} Belgian Rifle Battalion. One of the fusiliers fired his automatic rifle at the first pile, but the trace failed to ignite the gas. They then used their bayonets to pierce the cans and spread the gasoline over the next pile. The fire was then lit with a match. It was a Sunday afternoon. Before the fire, a large part of the German column of tanks and infantry entered the town and continued their attack westwards towards La Gleize. They never attempted to take the road north of Stavelot.*[19]

Leaving the three burning heaps, Lieutenant Detroz's men got back into the GMC and left in the direction of Francorchamps, after the GIs had taken over and burnt the other piles. It is estimated that 470,000 litres of fuel were burnt by the Belgian riflemen and the GIs of the 526th AIB.[20]

The Belgian riflemen set fire to the Haute Levée depot to prevent it from falling into enemy hands. (*Rights reserved via Laby*)

Pfc Jack Mocnik of the 526th AIB described what happened:

I think Captain Mitchell got permission to fall back and regroup, by this time the German tanks had crossed the bridge (this was the bridge the pioneers neglected to blow up, allowing the German tanks to run us over). Captain Mitchell, Lieutenant Wheelwright and I went out of Stavelot and up the road to the petrol depot. There were two Belgian soldiers (in English uniforms) at the start of the petrol dump and I think Wheelwright, who spoke a little French, tried to explain that when the last half-tracks overtook them they were to set fire to the dump. We then went back to Stavelot and started guiding the people and vehicles from Stavelot to take the road to Spa. What actually happened was that all but two of the semi-trailers went back to Malmedy. It was a bloody mess – the German tanks were on our side of the river. I had the jeep locked in four-wheel drive and the transfer case in gear, so I was going as fast as I could, hoping that no tanks would follow us because they would have sprayed us with their MGs. This four-wheel drive jeep with the gears down could only do a little over 50 mph. As we went up the hill where the gasoline depot was, we

The Haute Levée depot after the fire. (*NARA*)

came across the two semi-trailers; the men were firing 50-calibre and 30-calibre rounds at the jerry cans, but the gasoline never caught fire. The GIs jumped out and started opening the 5-gallon gas cans and finally managed to start one hell of a fire. Mitchell then told me to keep going. On reaching the end of the petrol depot we met Major Solis for the first time that day. There was about a quarter of a mile of fuel on fire, the damnedest fire you ever saw, the cans were exploding and flying through the air like a rocket, trailing fire and smoke.[21]

Change of Course in Trois-Ponts

KG Peiper then continued its progression towards the Meuse. It left Stavelot and went straight ahead, leaving the Amblève valley. It had to pass through a small town called Trois-Ponts, at the confluence of two valleys, the Salm and the Amblève. The town takes its name from its three road bridges: two spanning the Salm and the third the Amblève.

After winning a night in front of Stavelot, the American combat engineers would again play a crucial role in the battle. While his men were busy securing the heights of

The town of Trois-Ponts stood on Peiper's route. (*Esmalux*)

Stavelot,[22] Colonel Wallis Anderson commanding the 1111th Engineer Combat Group turned his attention to the defence of Trois-Ponts. At about 19:00 he called Lieutenant Colonel Fraser, commanding the 51st ECB, and ordered him to send a company to Trois-Ponts to help establish a coherent defence. He also requested additional supplies of demolition equipment, mines, bazookas and machine guns. At about 20:00, Fraser sent his C Company, located at Melreux, to Trois-Ponts.

The detachment was under the command of the Executive Officer of the 51st ECB, Major Yates. Its advanced elements arrived on the spot shortly before 23:30 and immediately started to prepare the demolition of the bridges over the Amblève and Salm rivers, while setting up roadblocks.[23] The 140 men of C Company were unaware of the importance of their mission[24] and especially of the imminent danger they were facing. Their firepower consisted of eight bazookas and ten machine guns.[25] They were reinforced by a 57-mm

Bridges were blown up right in front of Peiper. (*NARA*)

gun of the 526th Armored Infantry Battalion, which was immobilised on the spot. The half-track towing it had drifted to Aywaille. Helped out by a civilian, the machine found itself orphaned in the town of Trois-Ponts in full effervescence.[26] If the weapon was not powerful enough to pierce the front armour of a Panther, it was nevertheless able to immobilise it by a blow in the tracks. The delaying group was integrated into the city's defence. The weapon was placed in a battery at the exit of the first bend, just below the Trois-Ponts viaduct, in front of the first bridge over the Amblève. In addition to this meagre number of men, Yates had two squads from Lieutenant Bucky Walters' platoon, that of Staff Sergeant Paul Hinkel of A Company, 291st ECB and that of Sergeant Angelo Magliocca of C Company, 291st ECB. They were joined by other elements of the company, Lieutenant Warren Rombaugh and about twenty sappers from his platoon who arrived at the end of the day from Château de Froidcour. A breakthrough by the enemy always results in the dispersal of units, whose stray men retreat to the rear. A number of these stragglers arrived at Trois-Ponts on 17 December. They were added to the defenders' resources, but they did not bring a great deal to the table[27] to face the powerful armoured column that was heading straight for them.

The SS knew that its only chance of reaching the Meuse was to take advantage of the disarray caused by its surprise breakthrough and to exploit it as quickly as possible. At around 10.45,[28] its lead Panther appeared in front of the 57-mm gun. According to the official version of the US Army, the American servicemen did not lack composure. They managed to disable the lead armour with a direct hit. The German retort was not long in coming; a 75-mm explosive killed the intrepid American defenders. The few seconds they had gained gave the Engineers time to blow up the bridge over the Amblève right in front of Peiper..[29] In fact, it seemed that the Panther stopped to give the Panzergrenadiers time to remove a string of mines placed across the road and the anti-tank gun fire had nothing to do with stopping the German column.[30] For Peiper, this was a bitter setback. He was at the head of the 6. Panzer-Armee with his flanks completely exposed. His column stretched for 25 kilometres and he was unable to contact his rear to coordinate the development of his attack.[31] He later told his American interrogators: '*If we had captured the bridge at Trois-Ponts intact and had had enough fuel, it would have been a very simple thing to cross the Meuse that day. Blocked at Trois-Ponts we continued on to La Gleize, where we met with little resistance. There was another important bridge near Cheneux...*'[32] Thus, the initiative of the American engineers provoked a change of route for KG Peiper.

This was a good move, because if his Panthers had been able to continue straight on, they would have come across the flanks of the 82nd Airborne Division's truck columns in full transfer. A catastrophe was thus narrowly avoided by Anderson's initiative... If the gods of war were on the side of the American paratroopers, the danger was only postponed by a few hours. After crossing the Amblève at Cheneux, the diversions to Trois-Ponts meant that the KG Peiper had to cross the Lienne. The classes of the few bridges in the region left it little choice, and the torrent could only be crossed at Habiémont. Following this route out of the steep valley of the Lienne, the SS would inevitably arrive at the Werbomont junction. At the exact spot where the trucks of the 82nd Airborne Division were expected in the evening...

A Difficult Day

The Peiper column was forced to change course and was now headed for La Gleize–Cheneux; a decision which saved the American front. After the explosion of the bridges on 18 December, not much happened in Trois-Ponts. The sappers holding the town exchanged sporadic fire with the German elements passing under their noses, but the defenders could do nothing more. They had no heavy weapons and the isolated Americans, in a weak position, had no interest in provoking too strong a reaction from the enemy. They were forced to wait and hope.

Late at night on 18 December, with no reinforcements, Major Yates decided to try a ruse to make the Germans believe that the town was amply defended. He gathered his eight available trucks and gave them to Sergeant Magliocca's squad. He sent them up

American tactical aircraft attacked KG Peiper at Stavelot and Cheneux. (*NARA*)

The Dumont house above Cheneux was destroyed in the air attack. The civilians inside were killed. (*NARA*)

a hill with no lights, then down the hill with the lights on, then up the hill again with no lights, and so on until dawn. His aim was to make it look as if reinforcements were constantly arriving. Fortunately for Major Yates and his small detachment, the Germans turned away from his positions. There was no immediate need to take Trois-Ponts. Throughout 19 December the Germans returned sporadic fire from the sappers, but they remained out of range beyond the wet cutting.[33]

As Peiper reached Trois-Ponts after a lightning breakthrough at Stavelot, it became of paramount importance to support the efforts of the 1. SS-Pz-Div to advance westwards as quickly as possible and not to give the enemy time to build a solid line of defence. The interceptions of the radio traffic of the American military police allowed the Germans to analyse what was happening on the Allied side: many troops were coming down from the Aachen sector between Verviers and Liège.[34] For the moment, they only detected a part of the movements: the 7th Armored Division (AD), engineers and anti-tank units. There were, of course, many more. General Collins' VII Corps was about to move in including

The Panther damaged at Cheneux was used as a target after the battle. (*Rights reserved*)

Another view of Panther 131. (*Rights reserved*)

the powerful 2nd and 3rd AD, in addition to the 30th ID, the XVIII Airborne Corps with its 82nd and 101st Airborne Divisions was also on its way to stem the German advance. They took up position in a very favourable sector for defence and could not be driven out.

On its flank, the German armoured column was spotted by the Piper-Cub observation planes stationed at Spa airfield.[35] The cloudy weather with sudden breaks in the sky allowed a few sorties by the fighter-bombers of the 365th Fighter Group known as Hell Hawks, equipped with P-47 Thunderbolts. The forward point of the 1. SS-Panzer-Division was spotted at the entrance to the village of Cheneux. The intervention of the Thunderbolts caused panic in the armoured column, which subsequently stopped. When the tornado of fighter-bombers subsided, the damage was relatively minimal, but the loss of time, a good two hours, allowed the engineers of the 291st Engineers to mine the next bridge in Peiper's path. This bridge spanned the Lienne, a small river that is neither wide nor deep, but whose steep banks prevented any motorised crossing. The bridge once again blew up in front of the Panzer, and Peiper had no choice but to turn back and continue his search for a passage across the river out of the steep valley. It was a misty, overcast evening, and night fell quickly at that time of year. The weather was relatively mild, with temperatures ranging from 6.2 to 9.6°C.[36] The German troops set up camp in the woods bordering Château de Froidcour before launching the assault on Stoumont the following day. It was going to be a tough affair, as Peiper knew that the little town was defended.[37]

Chapter 10

The Last US Reserves Arrive

The Allied Response

So far this book has concentrated on the German breakthrough and the reactions of the American units involved. History has judged these front lines very harshly, and wrongly so. The two days they gained, trading precious seconds for their own blood, softened the impact of the surprise and allowed the Allied command to react and stem the crisis. Eisenhower had to throw in his last reserves to stem the German breakthrough. A race

At the time of the attack, the 30th ID was fighting in the ranks of the Ninth Army in Germany. (*NARA*)

against time began between the two adversaries. The arrival of the 7th Armored Division in the St. Vith area temporarily stabilised the situation in the northern sector of VIII Corps. However, Eisenhower knew that this point of his position was still under serious threat. The 1. SS-Panzer-Division progressed very dangerously towards the Meuse.

As soon as the US command realised that the German attack in the Ardennes sector might be a large-scale offensive, it detached reinforcements to the frontline troops in order to slow down the German advance. What he was aiming for above all was the protection of his lines of communication, in particular the Namur–Liège–Aachen axis.[1] The northern sector of the US system, spared by the last surge of the Third Reich's latest advance, was emptied in favour of the Ardennes. Consequently, from 17 December the Ninth Army transferred several divisions to its neighbour, the First US Army (FUSA). Among these means was notably the 30th Infantry Division (ID) 'Old Hickory'. The latter was relieved by the 29th ID at 20:30 on the evening of 17 December and immediately set off.[2] Uncle Sam's great elite unit moved with all its supporting armoured detachments, including the 743rd Tank Battalion (743rd TB) and the 823rd Tank Destroyer Battalion (823rd TDB). The venerable Old Hickory made the move from Germany to Eupen. From here, its sister regiments, 117th IR and 120th IR, moved towards Malmedy, while the 119th IR moved towards Remouchamps.

A Doughboy of 30th ID recalled these confusing moments: '*Around the 18th of the month we heard Axis Sally on the radio saying "30th Division guys get ready to pack your gear because Von Rundstedt has an armoured division that has penetrated your lines and is heading for your depot in Liège, Belgium."*'[3]

The 743rd TB was resting in the Kol Kellersberg Pattern area near the Dutch border. The unit was placed in reserve and took advantage of the opportunity for a complete overhaul. The 'Blues' were busy training in radio, map reading, tank tactics etc. Innovations were made, such as the tankers being trained in the use of the gyro stabiliser. In theory, this new system made it possible to fire the gun when the tank was in motion. However, this innovation did not appeal to the crews, who instead preferred to fire in a static position for greater accuracy.

In other welcome changes, the tanks were now equipped with 'Duckbill' track expanders. This adaptation, which widened the tracks, provided better traction thanks to a greater distribution of weight on the ground in muddy or snowy terrain. The crews also discovered a new secret weapon: a multiple rocket launcher mounted on the turret of the Sherman. The time was right to celebrate, as the first 48-hour leaves were being distributed. Others were taken by truck to Heerlen, Holland, to the Limburg Café, where a show by the 66th Air Ground Forces Dance Band and Dutch dancers delighted the Doughboys. Sadly, the good life of the garrison ended very quickly when the battalion was put on alert early in the afternoon of 17 December. Having had time to regroup its various units scattered in the region, the 743rd TB began its march at 02:00 on the night of 17/18 December.[4]

It is a well-known fact that the Germans knew about all American troop movements. When questioned after the war, SS-Brigadeführer Kraemer, Chief of Staff of the 6.

Duckbills were added to the Sherman tracks to improve mobility in the mud and snow. (*NARA*)

Panzer-Armee, stated that it was enough to intercept the radio messages of the US Military Police, as the vast majority of the radio messages were in clear text. As a result the Germans knew the destinations of every unit.[5] Private Kenneth C. Thayer was part of the K Company squad of the 119th IR. He recalled:

> *After being slightly wounded in the Aachen offensive in October 1944, I joined my brothers in arms of K Company, Third Battalion, 119th Infantry Regiment, of the venerable Old Hickory in Würselen, Northern Germany. At 15:00 on 29 November, Co. K embarked and was shuttled back to Kohlscheid, also in Germany, for a period of rest and recuperation after fighting in the bitter battle for the town of Pattern. We were resting, and after*

having breakfast on 16 December, we were told that a patrol was to be organised to search our front for an enemy parachute drop. Late in the day this unit came back empty handed. Our section was also told that we would be given another "90-Day Wonder"[6] *to replace Lieutenant Wonder, who was killed during the battle of Pattern. The name of the new officer was 2nd Lt. Mark R. Jolly. I never got to know him personally, as fate would have it. Rumours abounded of a great German offensive, the extent of which we could not yet imagine. The next morning, at breakfast on 17 December, worrying rumours began to take shape. It seemed that our stay in Kohlscheid would be cut short. We spent an anxious morning waiting for more precise news. Finally, in the early afternoon, all doubts were removed when 6x6 trucks arrived in our area. These vehicles were lined up in a convoy. Cries of "Get in! We're leaving!" echoed everywhere.*

We were given the usual fifteen minutes to roll up any non-essential equipment in our bedding. We then proceeded with the usual operation of gathering our equipment and depositing it in a pile outside our quarters, where it was collected by the supply sergeant and subsequently stored with the kitchen equipment. We assessed the situation. The 6x6s that had canvas cabs were open with the windscreens folded up against their bonnets.

On 17 December, the 30th ID was sent to urgently seal the gaps in the line. (*NARA*)

This is called a 'tactical configuration', which has the lowest possible silhouette. This was not a good sign. We were certainly not going to Paris! We had to climb aboard as ordered by the noncoms, taking with us our 30-calibre browning light machine guns and 60-mm mortars, as well as our front-line ammunition supply. Because of our exposure in the open vehicles and the bitter cold, we were instructed before boarding to wear all our clothing, which consisted of several layers, including long woolen underwear, olive drab woolen trousers and shirt, and a field jacket, topped with a long coat. We also wore a knitted woolen cap under our helmets and leather-faced woolen gloves. Nevertheless, we were already feeling the penetrating winter winds on this exceptionally cold day.

We learned later that our Regiment was the lead unit in the divisional convoy, probably because our regimental billets at Kohlscheid were the closest to our destination, which was still unknown to us at that time. It turned out that reconnaissance jeeps preceded us in the dark, in order to find us a suitable route, a hellish task for our leaders. This led to what we called the 'Caterpillar method' – the trucks would move forward a few lengths and

Arriving in Stavelot, the GIs of the 117th IR cleared the burnt jerry cans to let the TDs through. (*NARA*)

then stop, which happened every time a preceding vehicle accelerated or stopped, causing a chain reaction towards the rear of the convoy. Add to this the problem of trying to make out road signs and unfamiliar terrain with almost no lighting, as the trucks were only using their dim headlights. Only the use of low beam 'cat's eye' headlights was allowed. We moved slowly, stop and go... stop and go. Exposed to the elements, we were cold, shivering and shaking. We huddled together in the back of the truck trying to keep warm, but to no avail.[7]

Major General Gavin's Surprise

The paras of XVIII Airborne Corps under General Ridgway were also sent to the Ardennes sector. The two divisions to which they belonged were the 82nd and 101st Airborne Division (AbnD). The 17th AbnD was also part of the corps, but was still in training. General Ridgway was not on the Continent when his two veteran units were

General Ridgway was in England when the attack began. (*NARA*)

put on alert. Instead, he was in England, supervising the finalisation of the preparation of his division. Alerted urgently, he took off with the first plane for Reims.[8] As General Taylor, the commander of the 101st AbnD, was in Washington, it was up to the young leader of the 82nd AbnD, Major General James Gavin, to take immediate action to throw Eisenhower's last reserve into battle. The officer explained the circumstances of his unit's alert:

> *On 16 December 1944, the first signs of trouble in the Ardennes were announced as a small penetration on that front. I was worried because some of the troops in the Ardennes were very inexperienced and all very thinly spread. In effect they were placed there because they were trained as rookies to allow them to gain combat experience without imposing too much involvement … Early in the evening of 17 December, as I was dressing for dinner, I listened to the evening news on the radio. It sounded ominous. Serious German penetrations had been made in the Ardennes region. Knowing our weakness in this area and the shortage of reserves, I was increasingly worried. A few moments later, as I was having dinner with the staff at our house in Sissonne, I received a call from the XVIII Airborne Corps Chief of Staff. It was Colonel Ralph Eaton, former Chief of Staff of the 82nd AbnD and we were good friends. He told me I was the Corps Commander, General Ridgway being in England. This was a new thing for me as well, the XVIII Airborne Corps was the reserve of SHAEF. Of course I had to make the decisions and move the corps immediately if that was what SHAEF had ordered. But I was disturbed that I had not been informed earlier and, as far as I knew, we had no plan in place for the movement of the corps. Major General Maxwell Taylor was on leave in Washington and then Colonel Eaton told me that SHAEF considered the situation on the Ardennes front to be critical. Furthermore, the 82nd and 101st AbnDs had to be prepared to move within twenty-four hours of daybreak. He said that so far he had been unable to get in touch with General Ridgway. I told him to at least give orders immediately to the commanding general of the 101st AbnD, Brigadier General Anthony McAuliffe, to prepare immediately for movement in accordance with SHAEF's wishes. […]*
>
> *I had the staff assembled in the War Room, where the situation map with the latest information was displayed. Fortunately, the division was ready to move as we had already distributed four days' worth of ammunition and food to each of the regiments. We started the meeting around 20:00. It seemed to us that the main German forces were moving in the direction of St. Vith, which was still in our hands. At 21:30 I received another call from the Corps Chief of Staff, who told me that the Corps had been ordered to move in the direction of Bastogne, where further orders would be given. As Corps Commander I was to report to General Courtney Hodges, commanding the First US Army (FUSA), without delay. He was in Spa, Belgium. We prepared our movement orders. The soldiers were to be recalled. It appeared that the best time to march would be just after daybreak. This would minimise the confusion and we would arrive in the combat zone, hopefully before dark.*[9]

Major General Gavin took temporary command of the XVIII Airborne Corps. (*NARA*)

Really Ready?

From James Gavin's memoirs it appears that his division was perfectly managed and ready to go into battle immediately. In fact, the testimonies of some of his officers seem to indicate that at the Sissonne camp, the situation in his regiments was quite different. It should be remembered that the division had fought in Operation *Market Garden* and was only withdrawn from the front on 12 November 1944, barely a month before being put back on alert.

Thus Jonathan Adams, commanding officer of A Company of the 508th Parachute Infantry Regiment (PIR) said of morale, training and equipment:

> *The division was relieved at Nijmegen in Holland and sent to Sissonne in France. This camp was established in a French barracks. It was entirely logical to assume that the*

The 82nd Airborne suffered heavy losses in Holland. (*NARA*)

The paratroopers left Holland in November 1944. (*NARA*)

division had been withdrawn to prepare for an airborne assault across the Rhine in early 1945. This was eagerly anticipated, as many airborne officers felt that the services of this type of unit were wasted on missions other than airborne. When the division arrived at Sissonne, it was not immediately reorganised or re-equipped. In fact, the unit had a very low priority in the theatre. The equipment the division possessed was, for the most part, either salvaged or sent to troops fighting in Germany. Clothing and footwear had also been sent for repair, while the weaponry had been returned to the armoury for an absolutely necessary check. As there were no replacements available, the division had not yet been upgraded. The parachute schools in England had helped a little, but there were few volunteers for airborne service at that time. For the first few weeks after the division's arrival at Sissonne, training had been kept to a minimum and attention was given to

> *morale. Most of the time was used for sport, but every day there was also inspection and drill. As spit and polish was emphasised, the division gradually regained the discipline that is invariably lost in battle. For entertainment, a system of trips to Paris was instituted. US entertainers and French shows were brought to Sissonne. From about 1 December, the training became intense and it soon became apparent from their structure that this was for progressive preparation for an airborne jump.*[10]

At the 504th PIR, the situation was very similar, the unit being in the midst of a reorganisation after its fifty-seven-day operation in Holland. The second battalion also had an inexperienced S3,[11] a former commander of D Company, who had just been promoted.[12]

It should be noted that at Suippes, where the 505th PIR, the divisional artillery and the 80th Airborne Anti-Aircraft Battalion were located, the situation seemed to be better in terms of preparation. The units had their basic ammunition supplies and a sufficient level of rations had been maintained.[13]

Thus, on the whole, Gavin's division was in a state of unpreparedness, much like the 101st AbnD, although it seems that the artillery was better prepared. In any case, the parachute units were used to dealing with the unexpected and would get themselves in order in record time.

All Hell Breaks Loose!

After the staff meeting, the wheels of the division were set in motion. The delay accumulated during the rest period had to be made up in one night.

At the II/508th PIR, the battalion commander, Lieutenant Colonel Otho E. Holmes, called his company commanders for a briefing with a very vague outline: '*an enemy counter-offensive had broken through the front and the division had to go.*'[14] A little later, the instructions became clearer: '*Be prepared to move to Bastogne in Belgium by truck at 11:00 tomorrow.*'[15]

At the II/504th PIR, Lieutenant Colonel Edward Wellems gave slightly more precise information:

> *The Germans have made a breakthrough in the Ardennes sector near Bastogne. Some American units have already been overrun, especially the 106th ID. We will move tomorrow at 09:00 hours in 10-ton trailers. Lt Donnelly will distribute K-rations and ammunition to the companies tonight. A machine gun ready to fire will be mounted on each truck cab in case of air attack. Lieutenant Brown will be in charge of the rear echelon of the battalion. Each company will leave at least two men behind for this echelon. The cooks will initially stay behind as well. All weapons in the armoury will be returned to us before we leave.*[16]

As one of the officers of the 508th PIR said:

The camp at Sissonne welcomed the survivors of Operation *Market Garden*. (*NARA*)

> *At first it seemed an impossible task. The weapons were still in the armoury. Clothing requirements had not been met and there was virtually no winter clothing in the division. A K ration per man was issued and a basic regimental supply of ammunition was allocated. As if there was not enough confusion as it was, the Rifle Companies were issued with 30% replacements at 03:00 on 18 December. This meant assigning each man, checking his equipment, filling in the gaps, preparing new lists and briefing the men.*[17]

Despite the difficulties, the various regiments were ready on time and started in a staggered manner. The equipment taken along was inadequate, almost 10% of the men did not have helmets and many did not have their individual weapons. There were no machine guns without tripods or mortars without support. The important thing was that the paratroopers were ready to leave in record time, and this was indeed the case.[18] Initially, their destination was Bastogne, where they were to defend the town alongside the 101st AbnD, but things were to change in response to the situation on the Ardennes front, which was gradually getting worse.

Change of Course

While he left his unit to prepare, Major General Gavin travelled to Spa to receive instructions from General Hodges. Hodges was an officer he knew well and appreciated having served under him in the Philippines in the 1930s. After a gruelling night journey of more than ten hours, he arrived in Spa at 09:00 and received a report on the situation, which was not very encouraging. The left flank of Hodges' army was at Aachen, some 20 kilometres north of Spa. There were three corps in line. The VII Corps was in the north, V Corps in the centre and VIII Corps in the south. The whole area stretched over about 160 kilometres of front. The situation in the south was still fairly stable in the eyes of the First US Army staff, although the troops were heavily engaged. In the centre, two regiments of the 106th ID were surrounded. The possibility of delivering supplies by airdrop seemed impractical given the densely wooded terrain, the difficult weather and the degree of uncertainty as to the exact location of the troops.

It was in this difficult situation that Gavin and Hodges discussed the possible use of the XVIII Airborne Corps. Scanning the map for key positions to hold that would

Gavin went to Spa alone. (*NARA*)

slow the German advance, the Chief of Staff stopped at Bastogne. Many roads led from this town and its capture seemed essential to the continuation of the enemy offensive. Hodges therefore ordered that a division be placed there under the command of General Troy Middleton, head of VIII Corps. For the protection of the northern shoulder, the generals agreed on the hill overlooking the small town of Werbomont, 20 kilometres south-east of Spa. There was a good tactical reason for this choice: a crossroads between an important road running north-south and another running east-west. Holding this axis made it possible to prevent the enemy from reaching Liège. The various Allied staffs were convinced that this city was the objective of the offensive. It is true that it contained an important logistical centre and that captured German soldiers had confirmed that the slogan 'Liège by Christmas' was widespread in the ranks.[19] As the 82nd AbnD was leading the movement, Gavin ordered it to push on to Werbomont. The 101st AbnD, being further back, was directed to Bastogne. While the meeting was in full swing, a staff officer entered and delivered a field message to the Chief of Staff. It was one of those little yellow pieces of paper used by NCOs to send a message to a platoon leader or company commander. Gavin was struck by how unusual it was to ask an army commander to read such a message. It had come from a non-commissioned officer at an outpost in Stavelot, 13 kilometres away, reporting that a German armoured unit had arrived in Stavelot and crossed the Amblève.

The news hit like a bomb. Apart from the fact that the FUSA headquarters was practically on the front line, there was a huge army depot between Stavelot and Spa containing, among other things, over 2 million gallons of petrol. The German unit in question was none other than Kampfgruppe Peiper at the tip of the 1. SS-Panzer Division, which was crossing Stavelot and heading for Werbomont. Gavin was concerned:

> *It was almost as close to Werbomont as I was at the time and much closer than the 82nd AbnD, which was driving through Belgium in a lorry by an administrative type transfer. In our state of mind at the time it was difficult to see that the Wehrmacht, after being so badly beaten and having lost all their tanks, trucks and other equipment a few months before, would be able to mount a major offensive, especially in spite of the fact that we had complete control of the air at the time. No factory or industry could escape the enormous effervescence of our air power, as many believed. The German military*

General Hodges was in a critical situation when Gavin arrived in Spa. (*NARA*)

> *had survived – indeed was in better shape than any of us realised – and the 82nd AbnD was once again engaged against the Wehrmacht, this time in very strange and difficult circumstances.*[20]

By the time the FUSA had decided to change the location where the 82nd AbnD was to be committed, its regiments had already set off for Bastogne. The men piled up to sixty per trailer with supporting weapons. Battalions started at five-minute intervals. In general, it was the battalion's S3 jeep that led the way for the 240 kilometres from Sissonne (for the 508th PIR) and 230 kilometres from Suippes (for the 505th PIR and 80th Airborne Anti-Aircraft Battalion), the two camps being located on either side of Reims. The route passed through Charleville, Recogne, Sprimont, Houffalize and Werbomont. Stops were frequent and sometimes for futile reasons. The first formations arrived at their destination after 19:00 on 18 December, and the others followed in a staggered manner throughout the night.

Confusion at the Old Hickory

The 30th Infantry Division 'Old Hickory', dubbed 'Roosevelt's SS' after the terrible fighting at Mortain, Normandy, in August 1944, was one such infantry division sent to halt the German advance.[21]

The conditions of the transfer of the 30th ID were no more enviable. As we have seen, the men were cold and were moving in unloaded trucks to be ready to fight at the slightest alert. To make matters worse, the Luftwaffe was on the prowl:

> *Overhead was a German plane, universally known to GIs as the ubiquitous 'Bed Check Charlie', as we called this lone enemy plane that flew over our lines at night. We had air superiority and the Luftwaffe was all but gone. The war was over for them. Their staff believed so, but not Adolf Hitler. Charlie knew it too, but he had to follow his orders. Anyway 'Bed Check Charlie' paid us a familiar visit in search of our convoy. The enemy pilot dropped nine flares and then bombed and strafed us. We quickly jumped out of the trucks and dove into the ditches as was the procedure in case of an air attack. It was important not to turn our faces upwards as our pale skin reflected the flares or the moonlight. The enemy pilot was apparently blinded by his own flares as his bombs missed our convoy. We hastily got back on the trucks and set off again, somewhat warmed by our physical activity.*[22] *Hours later, in the indescribable cold, the convoy suddenly stopped. "Get off the trucks and take cover", we were ordered.*

The first elements crossed the Belgian border at Hauset around midnight and continued to establish themselves on an arc passing by Malmedy, Stavelot and Stoumont. These infantrymen were accompanied by the M10 tank fighters of the 823rd TDB. For the first time in the war, these ultra-mobile anti-tank units were to be employed in the doctrinal role for which they were designed: to establish a defensive front in the path of an armoured rush and destroy it. Although they shared a similar chassis with the

The GIs took up positions in the Lienne Valley to protect the deployment of the paratroopers. (*NARA*)

Sherman, they should be seen not as tanks, but as self-propelled artillery pieces. Our veteran, Private Kenneth C. Thayer, continues the story:

> *By the evening of 17 December we had advanced to the hamlet of Hauset, near Eupen, where we stopped for the night. This was only about 30 kilometres from our starting point near Aachen! Our assigned vehicle was in front of a farm. Our platoon set up in a barn filled with good hay. We proceeded to open our K rations and after eating, we settled down for a comfortable night's sleep. Someone else was assigned to take the first watch outside in the freezing weather. He would be relieved in an hour's time by the next unlucky person. Nevertheless, I was able to have a peaceful and uninterrupted night, as even 'Bed Check Charlie', in his JU-88, had returned home.*[23]

The Arrival of the Paras

The column of the 119th IR moved from Eupen to Verviers and ended up in Remouchamps. In the ranks, apprehension was building:

> *Early the next morning, 18 December, we were woken up and once again we heated up our K rations and ate a meal in a hurry. Then it was the classic 'hurry up and wait'. It wasn't until early afternoon that we climbed back into the refrigerated trucks and began another day of tedious travel, two or three truck hops at a time. The scout jeeps ahead of our convoy continued to try to decipher the road signs. For ordinary GIs like me, at this point, deployment orders were given from the division to the regimental and battalion commanders. Generals Hobbs and Harrison, the divisional commander and deputy commander respectively, had received bits and pieces of information from General Courtney Hodges, head of the First US Army (FUSA) in Spa. The general situation remained confused and fluid. This uncertainty proved to be a nightmare for senior officers and combat soldiers on the ground. Adding to this consternation, on 18 December we received our first contact with the prototype German V-1 'Buzz Bomb' cruise missile […] The sound of its ramjet, moving about 300 metres above our heads, was haunting and noticeable by the distinctive sound that echoed between the ground and the low clouds. Every minute one of these little beauties would pass over our convoy, heading for an objective in the rear unknown to us. Years later I learned that the Volkswagen Company produced these weapons of terror for about $600 each. We pressed on, negotiating deep gorges eroded by shallow, noisy streams and rivers with steep embankments. Hurrying along the narrow, winding roads, our drivers constantly hammered the gearbox of their lorries, up and down the steep terrain. The winter environment seemed so strange that we might as well have been redeployed to the Russian front! The whole ordeal was a source of extreme nervous tension, with the unknown purpose of our mission adding to our stress. We had no idea of the tragic gravity of the situation.*[24]

From Remouchamps, I and III Battalion went up the road next to the Ardennes river. The II Battalion was ordered to go to Werbomont to cover the arrival of the 82nd AbnD.

Reinforcements arrived just in time to shore up the engineers' positions. (*NARA*)

Arriving at its destination in the early night of 18 December, the regiment took up its defensive positions. The 1st Infantry Battalion of the 119th Infantry Regiment (I/119th IR) set up in reserve at the regimental HQ at the Halte de Lorcé along the Liège-Luxembourg railway line.

The II/119th IR rushed into the Lienne valley to cover the arrival of the 82nd AbnD's paratroopers, who landed at the Werbomont junction. The III/119th IR was given the hard task of stopping the advance of Kampfgruppe Peiper. The battalion arrived at Stoumont at about 21:00 and the GIs took up positions in the dark. Private Thayer stated: '*On 18 December 1944, at about 21:00, I arrived with other soldiers from the two light machine gun squads of 4 Platoon at our assigned defensive strongpoint. Located in a north-western corner of the outskirts of the village of Stoumont, which we later called Monville Farm.*'[25]

The III/119th IR, commanded by Lieutenant Colonel Fitzgerald, was understaffed. On 17 December in its three companies, the attendance list of officers and outfielders was as follows: I Coy = 145; K Coy = 137 and L Coy = 165. Nevertheless, the unit had its usual auxiliary detachments. In his memoirs Lieutenant Colonel Sidney Dettmer, commanding officer of the 823rd TDB stated:

> *A Company, minus the 2nd Platoon and Maintenance Platoon, was attached to III/119. The unit entered Stoumont, Belgium, at about 18:00 on 18 December 1944. An unknown number of enemy tanks were observed with their engines whirring about 1,200 metres south-east of the town. Immediate reconnaissance of the gun positions was carried out. The two Platoons moved into position, 1st Platoon under Lieutenant Thomas Springfield and the 3rd under Lieutenant Ward Jacobson, to the east, south and west of the town. Two mine belts were laid in a field along the road to La Gleize. At about 01:00 the Germans sent a small vehicle towards our lines along the main road to Stoumont. It advanced almost to the first minefield, stopped and then withdrew without damage. At about 04:30 on 19 December 1944, the same manoeuvre was attempted but this time the vehicle, a jeep, hit a mine and was destroyed.*[26]

The 1st and 3rd platoons had a total of eight towed anti-tank guns, seven of which were 76.2-mm (3 inch) from Uncle Sam and a Pak 40 7.5-cm from the German army. The battalion had been undergoing a major restructuring since 1 December, with the replacement of the towed guns with M-10s. The missing artillery pieces had not been replaced, so the gunners did not hesitate to 'requisition' German anti-tank guns, two of which were included in the company's official inventory.[27] Three towed 57-mm anti-tank guns from the battalion's organic staff company were included, but they did not yet have hoofed shells and were ineffective against the Wehrmacht's heavy beasts. The anti-tank arsenal had to receive additional support from two 90-mm guns of the 143rd AAA Gun Battalion.

These powerful artillery pieces were designed for anti-aircraft fire due to their tight trajectory firing qualities and high muzzle velocity. These firing specifications made it

The 119th IR had eight towed anti-tank guns, seven of which were US 76.2-mm (3-inch) and one Pak 40 7.5-cm, which was found at Stoumont after the battle. (*NARA*)

an excellent anti-tank gun. Unfortunately, it took an extremely long time to set up in battery, which fatally reduced its movement. Its bulk, height and lack of armour against battlefield scrap also made it easy prey to enemy infantry, which is why, where possible, a bulldozer needed to be provided to erect a protective parapet. During the Battle of the Bulge, Uncle Sam made the decision that the 90-mm would be used in anti-tank mode if necessary and in an emergency.

The two 90-mm guns sent as reinforcements came from C Battery, 143rd AAA Gun Battalion, under the command of Captain Leon Kent. At the annual veterans meeting on 20 July 2003, Leon Kent made the following statement:

> *On arrival at the 119th IR CP, 30th Infantry Division, I reported to Colonel Sutherland. We were attached to his unit. The Colonel told me he wanted two guns at Stoumont, and I sent Lt McGuire up there with two guns and the other two at junctions. Sutherland (119th IR* Commander) *asked me to stay with him as his liaison officer. Early the next morning I learned that one of my guns and McGuire had been lost. I only found out later what actually happened. On the way the gun got bogged down; they had followed the standard procedure to get it back on the road including a winch. Everything was going well, but when they started up, they were so excited that they forgot to disengage the winch and it was a disaster, everything got stuck and the gun was irreparably damaged and lost.*[28]

The remaining gun was placed in the village near the church. Uncle Sam's voltigeurs arrived at nightfall, and the companies were placed as follows: L Coy, commanded by

A 90-mm AA gun was lost during the push forward. (*NARA*)

Lieutenant Knox, took up position in the north of the town at a place called Le Rouat, where it was supported by the three 57-mm guns of the Staff Company. I Coy occupied the centre of the village and was supported by four 3-inch guns belonging to the 1st Platoon, under Lieutenant Thomas Springfield. The 90-mm gun in anti-tank mode was under Lieutenant McGuire.

K Coy, the least supplied with combatants, numbered 137 men and occupied the southern part of the town. It was supported by 3rd Platoon anti-tank unit commanded by Lieutenant Ward Jacobson, two of its artillery pieces were stationed near Monville Farm at the southern end of the town.

The 197th Field Artillery Battalion (Towed Howitzers) was commissioned to defend the II/119th IR in position between Werbomont and the River Lienne and to defend the III/119th IR at Stoumont. It settled on the heights of Nonceveux, 8 kilometres

Shermans of the 743rd TB supported the 30th ID in the area. (*NARA*)

away as the crow flies. The 400th Armored Field Artillery (self-propelled guns) was not yet in place. Moreover, the fire observers of these two units were not in the area either. Lieutenant Colonel Fitzgerald's GIs would not have the valuable support of the terrifying fire strike of the 105-mm batteries during the SS troop rush.[29] The men in olive-drab were in a delicate situation. They entered Stoumont in total darkness, no one had a clear idea of the terrain. The foxholes were hastily dug out and the anti-tank guns were embossed on the spot.

As soon as the battalion commander had settled in, he ordered a patrol to locate the enemy; at 21:45 it reported the presence of about thirty enemy tanks. The Germans were singing, talking loudly and smoking as if they were unaware of the presence of a nearby American unit.[30] The SS troops of Kampfgruppe Peiper bivouacked in the woods surrounding the lovely Château de Froidcour. The next day, at dawn, they launched an attack on the town of Stoumont. The cavalry of the 743rd Tank Batallion (743rd TB) was called to the rescue, and C Coy, with 111 troops and 6 officers, set off on 18 December at 03:30. It left Germany and joined the battalion on the way and went on the defensive at Xhoffraix in Belgium. The Sherman-equipped C Coy and the M-5-equipped D Coy were ordered to rush to Malmedy. At 21:00 it was attached to the 119th Infantry Regiment and had to join it via Francorchamps, Spa, Theux and Remouchamps. From the city famous for its caves, the 3rd Platoon, with its five Shermans, went to Werbomont to reinforce the II/119th IR in the Lienne valley. The ten Shermans of 1st and 2nd Platoon continued towards Stoumont. At about 05:30 on 19 December, the tankers had been on the road for twenty-six hours, so a little rest was needed and the troops bivouacked at the Halte de Lorcé, where the regimental HQ was installed.[31] After a brief respite of one hour, the Shermans set off again towards Stoumont, where the situation turned into a nightmare.

Like in Hollywood movies, the cavalry arrived just in time, fifteen minutes before the fighting began. The tanks arrived at full throttle, pressing fast and hard to increase the operational responsiveness of the GIs, and they moved into position immediately.

The ten Sherman tanks of 1st and 2nd platoons were under the responsibility of Lieutenant Walter D. Macht, recipient of the Silver Star Medal, which he had won heroically in October in Germany. Sherman's 1st Platoon took over the defence of the hamlet of Le Rouat to the north of the village in support of L Coy. Meanwhile' 2nd Platoon embedded itself in order to block the main road which crossed Stoumont and the middle of the village. Each platoon left a tank in reserve in the centre of the village.

A Risky Deployment...

In the early evening of 18 December, Major General Gavin suddenly realised the risks he was putting his men at by this transfer. In the afternoon, after conferring with Hodges, the leader of the 82nd AbnD went to Werbomont to reconnoitre his division's deployment area. He quickly identified the danger to his men:

I arrived at Werbomont about mid-afternoon and immediately reconnoitred the whole area. It offered excellent possibilities of defence. During my reconnaissance, I went down to the foot of the hill towards Habiemont. There I met a lieutenant with a detachment of engineers. They had prepared the heavy masonry bridge over the Lienne for demolition. A number of civilians carrying clothes and bedding were coming down the hill from Trois-Ponts. They were animated and all said that the Germans had passed Trois-Ponts and were heading in that direction. I went along the Lienne towards the Amblève and found no sign of the enemy. However, I did find a small intact bridge near the town of Forges. This was about a quarter of a mile from the main bridge at Habiemont. It did not seem to be strong enough to take heavy tanks. Nevertheless, when I got back to Habiemont, I asked the lieutenant about it. He said that he needed all the explosives he had to blow up the Habiemont bridge and that he could not use any for the bridge I had found; besides, he did not think it was an important bridge. Satisfied that I had done about all I could do before the troops arrived later that evening, I decided to go south to Bastogne and give General McAuliffe his orders in person. Also, I wanted to find out more about what was really going on in VIII Corps.[32]

Disembarked at Werbomont, the paratroopers crossed Rahier in the direction of Cheneux. (*NARA*)

Gavin had actually spoken to Lieutenant Al Eldestein of 291st ECB. The latter belonged to A Company, whose command post was located in Werbomont. It was Colonel Anderson himself who, after having analysed the map, understood the importance of the bridge over the Lienne at Neufmoulin[33] and ordered its destruction as soon as the first enemy came along.[34] Although he did not have the equipment to destroy the second bridge, Eldestein did not remain idle and sent a handful of fighters to Forges to mine the exit of the bridge identified by Gavin in order to hold back any enemy incursion there.[35]

After the reconnaissance of his release zone, Gavin went to Bastogne to VIII Corps headquarters. On his way back to Werbomont, he passed through Houffalize, where civilians told him that German armoured elements had just passed near the town.[36] One can imagine the stress that the general had to overcome at this precise moment, knowing that his deployment was threatened by the Peiper breakthrough. Yet there was nothing he could do now. His orders had been given, his division's trucks were on the road, unreachable and unable to defend themselves in case of an unexpected encounter with a German armoured column. Fate was on the march, and Major General Gavin had to keep his fingers crossed that night…

Chapter 11

Contact in Full Deployment

Danger Approaches

General Ridgway gave Gavin a tough assignment. (*NARA*)

As Gavin learned about the defensive possibilities of the region, KG Peiper continued to make progress. La Gleize was crossed on 18 December at 13:00, with no resistance having been encountered since Trois-Ponts. Nevertheless, between 14:00 and 16:00, after it had just crossed the bridge over the Amblève north of Cheneux, the column was attacked by the Allied air force without let-up.[1] The area was a large grassy expanse with very little cover: a tiny wood and coppice.[2] The German column was forced to remain stationary until dusk, but started up again at about 16:30. The preparation for the destruction of the Neufmoulin bridge over the Lienne had just been completed and Peiper's tanks arrived on site at 16:45. Spotting activity near the bridge, the lead tank opened fire, dispersing the Engineers. Corporal Chapin jumped into the hole where the detonator was located. His gaze met that of Lieutenant Eldestein, two steps away, who signalled him to blow up the structure. Chapin turned the key to the detonator, igniting the 1,133 kilograms of TNT that had just been set.[3]

The banks of the Lienne were so steep that the small stream served as an anti-tank ditch. Shortly before approaching the Neufmoulin bridge, Peiper ordered some SS-Panzergrenadiere mounted in SPWs to test the two bridges above Neufmoulin. One part crossed the Lienne stream on a dilapidated wooden bridge west of the Rahier border, and the other continued north-west of Chauveheid to the Forges bridge. All SPWs finally joined forces to pass Forges and headed south towards the N-23 road. Nestled in a ditch on the side of the road halfway between Forges and Neufmoulin, Private Johnny Rondenell heard the sound of approaching vehicles. He quickly set up his string of mines on the narrow road, barely having time to set up his device before the lead vehicle drove over it, detonating some of the mines. Private Rondenell sank into the thicket while the

The depots were strongly defended. (*NARA*)

SS fired in all directions. The leading SPW was destroyed, while the others ventured further in the direction of Werbomont until they came across two tank destroyers posted on the heights of Habiemont.[4] These belonged to A Company of the 823rd TDB,[5] who were supporting the 2nd Battalion of the 119th Regimental Combat Team of the 30th Infantry Division deployed around Habiemont to cover the arrival of Gavin's division. They, too, had only just moved into position.[6] Several German half-tracks were destroyed in the process and the survivors of the German reconnaissance column went straight back over the Forges bridge, informing Peiper that the bridge was impassable to the tanks of his KG.

A Tense Line-up

During the night of 18/19 December, the various regiments of the 82nd AbnD arrived from 20:00 and would spread out until the early morning. The last units were still on the road during the following night. The fighters arrived in dribs and drabs in the combat zone, one of them describing his state: '*A little before dawn on the 19th, frozen, dry, exhausted, the 82nd disembarked near Werbomont...*[7] The drivers were getting tired and the risk of mistakes was increasing. A platoon leader of the 80th Airborne Anti-Aircraft Battalion (AAAB) in the last convoys explained:

> *At about 01:00 hours on 19 December, after stopping for several minutes, the platoon leader got out of his vehicle and started walking towards the front [of the column] mainly to get some exercise and warm up, but also to ascertain the reason for the long delay. He was also curious to know where the division was going. After passing fifty or sixty vehicles, asking questions of the occupants of the vehicles as he went along without learning anything new, he arrived at what appeared to be the lead vehicle. The driver and co-driver were asleep in the cab. They had dozed off and did not know how far the truck in front of them had already gone. The platoon leader got into the truck and started the column again. This was a stressful moment for him, he did not know where the column in front of him had left from or where the division was going. His anxiety vanished when after twenty-five minutes of driving, the column he was temporarily guiding caught up with the vehicles in front. After admonishing the driver to stay awake, he got out of the truck and waited for his vehicle to get in.*[8]

This episode says a lot about the fatigue of the crews and the pressure on the managers to bring their contingents to safety. It is important to underline here the luck of the American airborne division during its transfer. Houffalize was bypassed by the 116. Panzer-Division, believing it to be heavily occupied. The large German unit arrived south of the town on the evening of the 18th and did not attack until the following day,[9] just after the paratroopers had passed through. The last trucks towing the divisional artillery did not cross the town until the night of 18/19 December. This equipment, by its very nature highly vulnerable, could not have been saved.

As they arrived, units were placed on the defensive around Werbomont and reconnaissance was sent out to identify the enemy's position. The location was perfectly chosen according to General Ridgway. He arrived there on 19 December and wrote in his memoirs:

> *I found Gavin at Werbomont, which was not a town at all, but a small abandoned crossroads with a small two-storey farmhouse as its only dwelling. Only one battalion of the 82nd AbnD had arrived. The rest of the division was rolling down the roads, moving as fast as the fog and muddy roads would allow. With his usual good initiative, Gavin had been on patrol, carrying out extensive reconnaissance to find the enemy who we knew were moving, somewhere, in the snow and fog. When other elements of the division started to arrive, I set up my forward CP in the farmhouse and we operated from there for five or six days. I doubt if a corps combat CP had ever operated in such a small area before, but there was nothing else to do.*
>
> *The 82nd AbnD arrived, battalion by battalion, and each element as it arrived was pushed forward to make contact with the enemy. But we had over 25,000 yards to cover*

with this one division and to my delight a magnificent fighting unit, the 3rd Armored Division (AD), was assigned to my Corps to help us fill this gap.

The 3rd AD was far away and came in piecemeal, and in my concern to make contact with its main elements and rush them, I set out long after dark to find them. I soon found myself in Theux, a Belgian town of considerable size, but completely dark and deserted, and as I wandered the dark streets, looking for someone to ask about the roads, I happened to see a beam of light coming through a crack in a door. I approached cautiously, not knowing if I had stumbled upon a German bivouac, and saw with great pleasure that the half dozen men in the room were GIs wearing the angular badge of the 3rd AD. They were members of a reconnaissance platoon who were themselves lost and were trying to locate their position on a map. But they knew the road their division was heading down, and they guided me back to Combat Command.[10]

The Rosier Depot

KG Peiper was beginning to run out of fuel. After passing the Haute Levée depot in Stavelot, it next passed the Rosier depot, one of the largest in the FUSA containing 2,226,000 US gallons.[11] The evacuation started on the night of the 18th and ended on the morning of 22 December, with no losses.[12] Almost the entire POL stockpile was saved thanks to remarkably efficient logistics, with the US administration declaring the loss of 124,000 US gallons (470,000 litres) of petrol.[13]

In a debriefing, Peiper stated that two trains loaded with petrol had not arrived for the offensive: '*Orders were given to all units to supply captured petrol. SS divisional intelligence had located two large depots Stavelot and Büllingen.*'[14]

Büllingen was part of a division of Gerow's V Corps, and Peiper seized 200,000 litres and refuelled his vehicles there.[15] Peiper contradicts himself regarding the Stavelot depot, stating that the intelligence service knew about the presence of a fuel stock in Stavelot and claiming the opposite a few minutes later. The facts are as follows: at that moment, the Kampfgruppe had refuelled in Büllingen and did not need more fuel, as a good soldier, the Obersturmbannführer blindly obeyed orders and progressed as quickly as possible without wasting time or taking the precaution of flanking.[16]

On 18 December, Lieutenant Walter Butts, a radio communications specialist, was ordered to move with his team in front of the fuel depot at Rosier. The radio team consisted of a driver and his assistant, and three radio technicians in a half-track. They arrived at the crossroads at around 10:00 and reported the situation to the First US Army HQ. Shortly after their arrival, they identified in the distance the sounds of a column moving through the valley[17] and perceived German flak fire towards Allied fighter bombers. The commotion seemed distant and did not alarm the Americans. However, at about 20:00 the men started to hear more identifiable sounds: heavy tanks were approaching!

As the petrol depot could not fall into the hands of the SS, reinforcements were requested and the general staff sent an anti-aircraft unit.[18] Lionnie Speer was one of the reinforcements and wrote:

The 90-mm guns took up positions to defend the roads. (*NARA*)

We set off at 02:00 on 19 December. We travelled along a steep and narrow mountain road under strict conditions of darkness. We took up this road about 4 or 5 miles south of Spa, just past the turn-off to Andrimont, where millions of gallons of petrol – the largest supply depot of the First Army – were stacked in jerry cans. There was a stack of cans every 50 yards or so. An American Tank Battalion had passed through and hit a number of the stacks, crushing enough cans that the petrol ran like water down the side of the mountain. There was a thick fog over the area and gasoline fumes permeated the air. We were all afraid that a truck would backfire or that someone would light a match and set the petrol on fire. The convoy was moving very slowly. We drove in the dark along a narrow dirt road, part of which was occupied by 5-gallon gasoline cans. Arriving at the crossroads to be defended, we set up our weapons, two 90-mm guns belonging to our unit, we were supported by elements of the 639th AAR armed with M51s.[19] *We were to be reinforced by a section of infantry from the 30th Infantry Division at 09:00 hours, they did not come.*

Sergeant Thomas Monahan returned from patrol and reported that a number of enemy tanks and infantry were moving towards our position. By noon Sergeant Ernest F. Breit, in charge of the section, was sitting on an M51 trailer, from where he could see the enemy across a small clearing. Orders were given not to fire and to let the Germans approach.

A Maxon Mount trailer was equipped with four 12.7-mm machine guns. (*NARA*)

> *At 15:45, when the first vehicles of the German column were finally in sight, an excited M51 gunner fired. The Germans returned fire. We did not fire our 90-mm guns because the Germans were below us and the 90-mm gun cannot fire below the horizontal. The first German vehicle coming around the bend immediately responded to the quad-50 fire. Several German shells pierced the shield and tore off the top of the gunner's head. He was killed instantly and Breit was wounded in the chin. The fight lasted only fifteen minutes. Then the enemy column consisting of an armoured vehicle, two half-tracks, a light tank and six semi-trailed vehicles withdrew to the road to La Gleize. It was assumed to be an armoured reconnaissance team. The battery report states that one enemy tank and one half-track were heavily damaged and several enemy killed.*[20]

KG Knittel Fights through Stavelot

The 1st platoon of C Company, 1st Battalion 117th Infantry Regiment (IR), joined the precarious roadblock of the 526th AIB at about 13:00 on 18 December. It descended towards Stavelot and with its long-range fire, took out boxes on the tail of Kampfgruppe Peiper. The M10s hit the mantle of Tiger No. 105, which ended up buried under the rubble in the Rue du Haut Rivage.[21]

The reconquest of the city had begun.

The I/117th IR attacked from the northern heights of Stavelot towards the town centre, which they found weakly defended and had managed to recapture two thirds of it by 16:00.[22] Intensive fighting took place in the area of the market square in particular.

The town of Stavelot came under German artillery fire. The church seen here was shelled. (*Stavelot Library*)

The five Shermans of 3rd Platoon of B Coy, 743rd TB were to support A Coy, I/117th IR at Stavelot. After a restless night, where the crews had not slept a wink due to constant air raid alerts and enemy parachute drops, 3rd Platoon arrived at the objective at 16:00. The 85 km long journey had taken its toll on the Sherman B17 and B19, which were damaged and remained behind for repairs. On the spot, Lieutenant Murray commanded the 1st Platoon of A Coy, whose small unit had to block any progress into Stavelot from the market square. This square is situated in the heart of the town and is a rectangle 75 metres by 40 metres.

Lieutenant Murray learned that half of the city was in the hands of the 1. SS-Panzer-Division. The officer of the 30th ID took things in hand, placing the Sherman B15 at the top of the square at the entrance of Rue Chaumont, with the B16 on the right, and the B18 is in reserve in the Rue Haute. Exhausted by a sleepless night, the American crews took a well-deserved rest in the houses bordering the square. On the other side of the Amblève, a good part of the Schnelle Gruppe Knittel, delayed and disorganised by the

The 743rd TB went up in line from the German-Dutch border. (*NARA*)

The small square in Stavelot was the scene of a violent confrontation. (*Rights reserved*)

intervention of the fighter-bombers, set off again from the south-east heights of Stavelot. SS-Sturmbannführer Knittel took the precaution of protecting his right flank during the crossing of the city and sent troops towards the market square.

At about 20:30 a dozen SS troops entered the square and moved towards the B16. The Sherman was guarded by Sergeant Ernest Kirksey and another GIs with whom he was talking to outside the tank. Seeing the threat, they fired their weapons at the attackers, which raised the alarm. The sergeant climbed onto his tank to grab the turret gun, while heavy fire stopped and drove back the mass of attackers. An SS man was left on the ground at the corner of the Rue de la Fontaine. Awakened by the shooting, the tankers quickly rejoined their vehicles and set them in motion. Shortly after this clash, Knittel sent in two SPWs of Heinz Wagner's 4. schwere Kompanie. The first came from the Rue Vinave and had hardly arrived on the square when the B15 placed near the Rue Chaumont fired with an explosive shell. At a distance of 50 metres, the Sd.Kfz.

This Sd.Kfz. 251/9 was destroyed Stavelot's town square by gunner Ralph R. Hemke, a crew member of a Sherman of the 743rd TB. (*Rights reserved*)

251/9 had no chance of escape, and the shell went through the lightly armoured vehicle, killing the entire crew as well as their dog. The second half-track of the Schnelle Gruppe, seeing the sad fate of its brother in arms, decided to turn back and follow the rest of Kampfgruppe Knittel towards Trois-Ponts.

The M10s gradually descended into the town and managed to take position on the right bank of the Amblève at the foot of the abbey at 18:00. From this position, they were able to stop the flow of reinforcements on their way to Peiper, as they took the bridge over the Amblève. Their report claimed the destruction of several armoured half-tracks.[23] Meanwhile, the 117th IR continued to reconquer the town. This was achieved after heavy fighting throughout the day on 19 December:

> *The regiment launched an attack southwards at 08:30 with the first battalion to capture and clear the south-western part of Stavelot and the part of the town south of the Amblève. The first battalion's attack initially made slow progress and at 08:50 a strong enemy counter-attack of armour and infantry was repelled. Advancing slowly, the battalion reduced all enemy resistance in Stavelot north of the Amblève and occupied defensive positions. Repeated enemy counter-attacks from the west and south-west were repelled throughout the day. At 19:30 a squad of men from A Company, 105th Engineer Combat Battalion, led by Captain Rice blew up the bridge. The Second Battalion continued to hold defensive positions on the heights to the north-east of Stavelot.*[24]

It should be noted that in the middle of the day, the M10s scored another hit by destroying a second Tiger tank near the bridge. The American reports are confirmed by SS-Gruppenführer and Generalleutnant der Waffen-SS Hermann Priess, commander of the I. SS-Panzer-Korps to which the 1. SS-Pz-Div was subordinated. He explained what this meant for his troops:

> *An enemy group had infiltrated south-east of La Gleize between the Gepanzerte Gruppe and the Aufklärungs-Abteilung and had interrupted the links with Peiper. The division committed its most advanced battalion of Marschgruppe 3 to re-establish the link. In the evening, the enemy attacked and pushed forward to the Amblève and interrupted the links again. Stavelot was obviously attacked from the north. At this point, the enemy hit the weakest part of the reconnaissance detachment, drove it back and retook the bridge. By a counter-attack of the Aufklärungs-Abteilung, the bridge was again in our hands, but during the evening the enemy took it back.*[25]

When the bridge was blown up in the early evening of 19 December, a vital artery for the communication lines of the 1. SS-Panzer-Division was cut off. Only a small footbridge over the Amblève near the bridge of the Petit Spay on the road leading to Trois-Ponts remained as a supply route for Kampfgruppe Peiper. However, this bridge was too fragile and collapsed when a Jagdpanzer IV tried to cross it.

M10 TDs took up positions in and around Stavelot. (*NARA*)

The 82nd Airborne Division

While he took the necessary steps to organise his XVIII Airborne Corps, General Ridgway gave Gavin the task of deploying his division in anticipation of the impending attack. He was initially to link up in the north with the 30th ID and in the south with the 7th AD at Vielsalm and St. Vith. In order to make the most of the daylight hours of 19 December, Gavin assembled all battalion commanders, as well as regimental commanders, at his divisional headquarters for the distribution of his orders. The 504th PIR was to deploy along the Amblève from Cheneux to Trois-Ponts. Patrols of the unit quickly made contact with the GIs of the 119th IR of the 30th ID.[26]

From Trois-Ponts, the 505th PIR took over to the south of Grand-Halleux. In the evening of 19 December, an engineer combat patrol coming from Trois-Ponts came across a paratroop of the 505th PIR coming from Werbomont through Haute-Bodeux and Basse-Bodeux. The encounter was mutually agreeable for both units, as the paratroopers expected to find Trois-Ponts in German hands and the sappers expected to find Germans on the road. At first light on 20 December, the forward elements of the 505th PIR moved to the heights west of Trois-Ponts. Just in time, in fact. Following the destruction of the Stavelot bridge, the SS used the concrete bridge at Petit Spay, although was barely strong enough to allow light vehicles to cross. Meanwhile, Trois-Ponts could

The 82nd Airborne Division set up positions to counter Peiper in the west. (*NARA*)

be attacked from the south if the SS managed to cross the Salm. So, although the bridge over the Amblève had been blown up, the little town remained important.

The 508th PIR took up position in Vielsalm, occupying Thier Du Mont to protect its western flank. The remains of the 325th Glider Infantry Regiment (GIR) were transferred to the divisional reserve. The regiments quickly left their defensive positions around Werbomont in the early morning darkness. There was so much uncertainty and rumour about the Germans that they were wary and moved forward very cautiously, to the extent that some units did not reach their final objectives until the following day. Gavin began to realise during the day that some of his troops had still not arrived at Werbomont overnight, in fact it would be several days before he had all his elements assembled. On 19 December the 325th GIR sent troops to Barvaux, about 18 kilometres to the west, and to Grandménil and Manhay, 13 kilometres to the south. The 505th PIR moved gradually from Habiemont to Basse-Bodeux and Trois-Ponts, while the 504th PIR moved towards Rahier. The 325th GIR, minus one battalion, was held near Werbomont in the divisional reserve.

On 19 December there were still many unknowns about the situation. All Gavin knew was that a panzer column seemed to be bottled up at La Gleize and that the 7th AD had carried out a brilliant delaying action around St. Vith, some 15 kilometres from Vielsalm. The manoeuvres of 19 December were therefore ordered by caution and aimed at obtaining information and making contact with the enemy, all in such conditions that the 82nd AbnD kept the initiative and remained under control, despite its immense dispersion.

Chapter 12

The Capture of Stoumont

Leading Forces of Kamfpgruppe Peiper

As previously discussed, the 119th IR of the 30th ID took position in Stoumont. With the bridge over the Lienne destroyed, Peiper had to move towards the Targon ford to have a chance of getting out of the Amblève valley. The 2. Komp of the I. SS-Panzer-Regiment 11[1] (2. SS-Pz-Rgt 1)[2] with eleven Panther Gs of the 2nd Panther company would take part in the attack, as well as two Befehlspanthers (command tanks). The first of these carried turret number 002 and was attached to Hauptsturmführer[3] Gruhle, Peiper's Adjutant.[4] The second, Panther 105, belonged to SS-Sturmbannführer[5] Werner Poetschke, who led the armoured regiment.

In preparation for the attack, the second Panther company (2. SS-Pz-Rgt 1) took the lead, allowing the first Panther company (1. SS-Pz-Rgt 1) to take a breather and reorganise in the village of La Gleize.

- Panther 201: Obersturmführer[6] Kompanieführer[7] Friedrich Christ
- Panther 202: Hauptscharführer[8] 1. Zugführer[9] Hans Friedrich
- Panther 211: Untersturmführer[10] Hubert Kaufmann
- Panther 214: Unterscharführer Rech
- Panther 215: Unterscharführer Krüger
- Panther 221: Hauptscharführer 2. Zugführer Heinz Knapich
- Panther 222: Oberscharführer[11] Walter Ropeter
- Panther 225: Rottenführer[12] Franz Prahm
- Panther 231: Untersturmführer 3. Zugführer Helmuth Koch
- Panther 232: Unterscharführer Herbert Brauschke
- Panther 234: Unterscharführer Herzog
- Four or five Panzer IVs from 6. Panzer-Regiment 1 were on site, following the Panthers in the second echelon
- Panzer 601: Obersturmführer Kompanieführer Benoni Junker
- Panzer 611: Untersturmführer 1. Zugführer Hans Steiniger
- Panzer 625: Oberscharführer Hubert Huber
- Panzer 631: Not known
- Panzer 634: Rottenführer Georg Eberhardt

In order to pool the objectives, the infantry supported the armoured units. For this purpose, Obersturmbannführer Peiper had at his disposal the third battalion III. (Gp.)/

The Panthers attacked Stoumont. (*Public domain*)

The Panzers were supported by powerful infantry. (*Public domain*)

SS-Pz-Gren-Rgt 2[13] of SS-Sturmbannführer Josef Diefenthal. This was the unit that Peiper commanded on the Eastern Front, and its nickname was 'The Torch Battalion', after its habit of systematically setting fire to conquered villages. Two sapper companies, the 3. (Pi)/SS-Pz-Rgt 1 commanded by Obersturmführer Franz Sievers and the 9. (Pi)/ SS-Pz-Rgt 1. of Obersturmführer Erich Rumpf supported the infantrymen.

These units were reinforced by an unknown number of Fallschirmjäger from 9. Fallschirmjäger-Regiment, requisitioned on the way.

The artillery was composed of disparate elements, notably the 1. SS-Pz-Art-Rgt 1[14] Howitzers (10.5 cm field howitzers) of the 13. (IG)/SS-Pz-Gr-Rgt 2.[15] equipped with six 15cm Grids. Some towed howitzers were able to keep pace with the Kampfgruppe.

The players in this drama of the Battle of the Bulge are well known. Captain Ferris, historian of the battle, describes the situation as follows: '*In fact, Stoumont was not easy to defend against an attack from the east. Tanks coming from that direction were not channelled, and could spread out over open ground, both north and south of the road.*'[16]

The attacker's view differed: '*Looking west from our position, the terrain to the left of the road sloped very steeply down to the cliffs above the Amblève river and it was impossible to deploy vehicles on this flank for the first 500 metres. To the right of the road was a gently sloping hill which hid the village until the very last moment. It was covered with fields, criss-crossed by barbed wire cattle fences*'.[17]

As a Panther entered Stoumont, the GIs withdrew under the cover of a smoke screen. (*Public domain*)

Stoumont is one of the few villages in the region that is not located at the bottom of the steep valley of the Amblève. It is situated on the northern slope of the watershed of the tortuous river, the settlement spreading out on the hillside in a gentle slope as soon as the escarpment to the south of the village is crossed. A Panzer could easily outflank the village on the northern flank, occupied by L Coy, and the southern flank defended by K Coy. I Coy, meanwhile, occupied the main road and its surroundings.

Looking at the planimetric map of Stoumont, Captain Ferris was correct. The town was difficult to defend as it could easily be overrun by the attacker via its northern and southern flanks. At first sight, the choice of defending the village was a tactical error, and the Kampfgruppe's advance could have been stopped easily a few kilometres downstream. From Stoumont, the invasion road to Liège ran along the river, and at this point, the left bank of the Amblève is lined with impassable cliffs. The road on the right bank is directly bordered by a dense and steep forest. Any overrun by the flanks was impossible for both infantry and tanks and it would have been more obvious to block the armoured column in this defile. The decision to stop Peiper at Stoumont is explained at the exit of the village: a road that gives access to the small town of Spa. The Americans did not know what the enemy's objective was, believing at the time that Peiper wanted to take either the town of Liège, where huge supply depots were set up, or the town of Spa, where the HQ of the First US Army was set up and moved to Chaudfontaine.

The Plan of Attack

The Panthers of Obersturmführer Christ's second company[18] had to lead the way in pushing the men of I Coy along the main road, State Route 33.[19] The half-track platoon, Sd.Kfz. 251/9[20] armed with a 7.5cm L24 gun of the 12. SS-Pz-Gren-Rgt 2 of Rudi Rayer followed closely, while the few Panzer IVs that were able to follow the Kampfgruppe remained in a second echelon.

The 11. SS-Pz.Gren-Rgt 2 of Obersurmführer Heinz Tomhardt was in reserve behind the tanks to finalise the assault. If the progress of the armour was stopped along the main road, they needed to outflank the GIs on the right side of the road and take them from behind via the hamlet of Rouat.

The south of Stoumont was to be taken by the Panzergrenadier of the 9th company of Untersturmführer Max Leike (9./ SS Pz.Gren.Rgt. 2), as well as the third pioneer company of Obersturmführer Franz Sievers (3./Pz. Pi. 1. Rgt.) and part of the Fallschirmjäger. This combat group set off from the Cheneux viaduct towards Stoumont along the right bank of the Amblève, at the level of the village where the troop needed to split. One group had to climb a steep slope to reach the southern part of the village defended by K Coy, the second group continued to the Targnon mill and up the road leading to Route 33 at the exit of the town to surround the III/119th IR. The northern part of the village, the hamlet of Rouat, had to be taken by the Fallschirmjäger, who then had to fall back at the junction of Route 33 and the road to Spa. The success of the attack depended on the neutralisation of the anti-tank guns and the encirclement of all US troops in the village.

SS and Fallschirmjäger fought side by side in Stoumont. (*Public domain*)

Panzer March!

At 08:00 the US observers saw a line of fifteen Panzers in place.[21] The Panzers warmed up their engines in accordance with standard procedure, and got into position for the morning assault.

At the head of the second section (2. Zug) Panther 225 (Rottenführer Franz Prahm) led the way. Being the least experienced of the section, he played the thankless role of the guinea pig. His Zugführer[22] (Heinz Knapich) followed him in Panther 221. Oberscharführer Walter Ropeter's 222 closed the second section.

The third section (3. Zug) was also strong, with three Panther Gs: 232 of Unterscharführer Herbert Brauschke in the lead, followed directly by his section leader Unterscharführer Helmuth Koch in 231, and Panther 234 of Unterscharführer Herzog.

Kompanieführer Friedrich Christ remained under observation (Panther 201).

SS-Sturmbannführer Werner Poetschke, commander of the Panzer-Abteilung, closed the march of the frontline attackers. In the second echelon, the first section (1. Zug) of Unterscharführer Rech's 214, Untersturmführer Hubert Kaufmann's 211, and Unterscharführer Krüger's 215 were waiting.

Peiper's adjutant, Hauptsturmführer Gruhle was in Panther 002[23] at the rear of the column and supervised the attack. At 08:30 anti-tank gun No. 1 was in firing position on the northern heights of the city and was neutralised by the Fallschirmjäger, who advanced in the mist. The artillery piece was subsequently abandoned.

A thick fog covered the battlefield as the Panzergrenadiere and the Fallschirmjäger marched towards the flanks of the American defenders.

At 08:45, German mortars fired a few rounds to soften the resistance of the US troops. The reports after the battle of the capture of Stoumont by the SS mention that there was no German artillery bombardment, only direct fire from tanks and mortars.[24]

Panther 225, which was in the front of the attack, is seen here in the background on fire, while infantrymen take care of the wounded. (*Public domain*)

Werner Poetschke led the assault on the town. (*Public domain*)

During an interrogation after the war, Peiper stated:

> *I arrived at La Gleize around midnight. I immediately ordered reconnaissance patrols towards Stoumont. The results showed that there were heavy enemy concentrations there. Thereupon I planned and prepared an attack in the early hours of the morning. Contrary to my first plan, I could not attack Stoumont at dawn, as there was a thick fog. The attack started at 09:00.*[25] *The terrain was very unfavourable. I could only rarely use my tanks. The enemy had dominant positions.*

It should be noted that the fog had lifted during the armoured attack, as can be seen from the photographs taken during the fighting. On the northern flank, at the hamlet of Rouat, the Fallschirmjäger came down from the forest towards the houses and started to neutralise the US anti-tank guns. South of the town, after having climbed the steep banks of the Amblève, part of the Panzergrenadiere, supported by Fallschirmjäger, took up position at the cemetery, where they were protected from small arms fire by the thick stone walls. The other group reached the Targnon mill along the river before climbing up to Highway 33, encircling part of K Coy at the St Edouard sanatorium.

Tuesday, 19 December 1944

As dawn broke over the commune of Stoumont, a thick fog covered the region, and the hell of the German attack was unleashed. The Panzergrenadieren, supported by paratroopers and armoured vehicles, launched an assault. For more than two hours, the fighting raged. Overwhelmed and partly surrounded, the GIs gave up and the city fell to the SS. The losses were heavy on the American side: all the anti-tank guns were lost and 267 men were missing, although fortunately the ten Shermans of the 743rd TB came through unharmed. The end of the fighting, however, did not mean that the Panzergrenadieren had come to a well-earned rest. At the Dachau trial after the war, Peiper said:

> *An artillery barrage started, which forced me to take cover. I gave instructions to my aide-de-camp, and he went to the exit of the village in a jeep with SS-Sturmbannführer Poetschke to meet SS-Sturmbannführer Josef Diefenthal, commander of the III. (Gepanzerte)/SS-Panzergrenadier-Regiment 2, to pass on my orders: to immediately follow the fleeing enemies and to make sure that all available vehicles increased the pressure on the fugitives.*[26]

At the 119th IR HQ, the bad news was piling up. Lieutenant Macht reported at 10:10 that he could not stay in Stoumont and that his Shermans had to give up ground. The III/119th IR reported that it was in danger of being surrounded. Colonel Sutherland, the regimental commander, decided to call in part of his reserve and ordered C Coy of the I/119th IR to rush to Stoumont to assist the III/119th IR. First Lieutenant Donald Strand recalls:

The Panthers here are at a standstill, blocked by a burning Panther 225. (*Public domain*)

> *I was given a mission at about 11:00 that day to reconnoiter towards La Gleize – to find the line of the 3e battalion. I came across a group of GIs retreating, spoke to an officer I knew and found it was total confusion. Later I found out that over a hundred GIs had been captured that day, I went back and reported to my battalion commander.*[27]

A Panzer IV from 6th Company moves around the Panther in flames in the garden of the Robinson house in Stoumont as it approaches the main street of the village. SS Grenadiers gathered along a hedge lining the main road as reinforcements moved towards the centre of the village from the south. Smoke from the destroyed lead Panther can be seen on the right. (*Public domain*)

Sergeant Curtis Martell's (C Coy) account confirms the mood at the time:

> *We got as close to the front of the German attack as we could before jumping off the trucks at about noon. We started up a hill towards the village. We didn't get very far before we saw a jeep with about ten men in it coming down the hill. Also, some of the men were on foot running away, one soldier even threw his rifle away. I was leading our column and needless to say we were alarmed at what was happening. The company commander ordered us to turn back. My second in command and I were at the rear of the column and we heard tanks on the top of the hill we had started from. The lead tank fired in our direction, the round hit a chicken coop near us and feathers were flying everywhere. We backed off and took up a position to fight.*[28]

Ray Haserodt, attached to the battalion's headquarters company, said:

> *We had the tanks and enemy infantry at our backs and were waiting for an order. When Sgt Ryan said the best thing to do would be to try and get as many men as possible in the jeep and trailer and 'jump'. Going down the hill, believe it or not, we had twenty-one people in the jeep and trailer. They almost rolled over. I was told, "Go for it!" And I accelerated as much as I could to get away. As we went down the mountain and I looked to the left, I was relieved and surprised that no German tanks were firing at us; I think they were just surprised at our bursting in. Then I saw German soldiers ready to fire on us. We felt like a bird for the cat. One bullet went right between my legs, hitting Sgt Ryan, another bullet hit the back of the jeep. Miraculously, no one else in the jeep or trailer was hurt.*[29]

The Panthers blocked in the main street disengaged on the north wing of the village. (*Public domain*)

Scramble at III/119th IR

At 10:40 General Leland Hobbs, the divisional commander, was on the front line. He visited the Regimental HQ and, realising the imminent threat, promised Colonel Sutherland to do his utmost to get him the 740th Tank Battalion as reinforcements.[30]

SS-Sturmbannführer Josef Diefenthal, commander of the III. (Gepanzerte)/SS-Panzergrenadier-Regiment 2, watches as US prisoners pass by. (*Public domain*)

What remained of the III/119th IR withdrew by infiltrating into C Company. At Targnon, the reinforcing riflemen made contact with Lieutenant Macht's ten Shermans, which were without the necessary infantry cover. The teams merged to support each other and despite the lack of ammunition, the reformed unit gave ground in a slow and orderly retreat towards the regimental HQ. On the way they came across a 90-mm gun at Stoumont station, under the command of Captain Leon Kent, commander of C Battery, 143rd AAA Gun Battalion. He states:

At 07:30 No 2 gun was put into position at Stoumont. It was destroyed by a mortar grenade which landed in the half-track containing the ammunition. It was parked nearby, setting off its ammunition and the ammunition of the gun. I had not heard from the gun under Lieutenant Kay's orders, so I went in the jeep to meet him only to find that nothing had been done. Furious, I went to Stoumont to see the situation for myself. With my driver we went ahead, and in any case, we arrived at Stoumont. I knew Lieutenant McGuire's position, but the road was jammed with American troops coming down. We couldn't get up there, so I walked up.

It was up the hill, a slope, and I remember crawling across the field. That's where I was most afraid during the war. I didn't know if the field was mined or anything, and I was

After the assault, Peiper (seen here in a submariner's leather suit) spoke with his men. The celebrations were short-lived, however, as the fighting had to resume immediately. (*Public domain*)

The celebrations were short-lived for the men of KG Peiper. After drinking and eating all they could find in the houses of Stourmont, they knew the fighting would resume immediately. (*Public domain*)

going ahead, my driver was scared. But he was following me. I borrowed his bayonet, actually, to go ahead and check. I finally met McGuire and he told me what had happened. I met the men and said, "You've still got the M4 Tractor,[31] *pile in and follow me". So we started to go back and my objective was to find the first flat spot where I could position my weapon.*

We continued on, and I finally spotted this station which had flat ground. We were in the middle of a retreating column, and I never imagined that the Americans would withdraw in this way. We started to set up the artillery piece. We couldn't dig in, of course, because the ground was paved and we didn't have time to fortify it, which we usually did with sandbags. We *were placed on high ground, but the building served as protection. I noticed that there was a curve in front where I could maybe hit a tank laterally. Anyway, the GIs kept retreating, I don't know how long it took, and finally one guy, a captain in the back of a jeep, shouted at us, "We are the last ones, the next guys you see are Germans. We've got a Daisy-chain in the road" and he said, "Hold them, we'll be back with reinforcements." Well, I didn't see any reinforcements.*

Anyway, so we waited a bit and it wasn't long before we saw a tank, but instead of presenting its side, it was presenting its front. The tank had swung around before it turned so that it was only showing its most armoured front. We made a perfect target. I was standing on the platform right next to the gun, with the gunners on either side of me and with another in the rear I felt useless. The dark shape of the Panzer was about 400 yards away, and we opened fire. Our 90-mm shot startled me as it always does. We

In the Amblève valley, the 90-mm US guns were watching. (*NARA*)

destroyed it in seven rounds. I got down from my post and started passing ammunition. There was only one magazine, but there must have been two. A second tank followed close behind and tried to overtake the immobilised tank, but again we opened fire and destroyed this second tank as it manoeuvred, blocking the passage of other tanks. We had expended a total of eighteen shells and destroyed two tanks; an excellent score of which we felt proud.

If the other tanks were blocked, the same was not true for the infantry. We were soon caught under machine gun fire, which neither destroyed the equipment nor wounded the men. The machine gun was neutralised by our fire, in this case the point 50 mounted on the M4 Tractor. A second machine gun targeted us, it was well concealed and it was impossible for us to hold the position. We destroyed our weapons and came down on our fourth and only remaining artillery piece. They had all sorts of anti-tank guns and tanks in there. It was in this action that PFC Donald Eyanson was killed and Pvts D.P. Phillips and Charlie Schofield were seriously wounded.[32]

The Panther destroyed by the 90-mm ambush at Stoumont station was Walter Ropeter's No. 222. He escaped with severe burns on his hands and face, and it was thanks to his leather suit that he was not completely burnt. His two companions in the turret, Schaten the gunner and Strasdin the loader, were seriously injured. The two other men were less lucky: the radio man Mathebowsky and the driver Schaudin were both killed in the confrontation.

The wounded were taken to the field hospital set up at Château de Froidcour. On Tuesday morning (19 December) a medical team requisitioned the château's dining room as it needed a large, clear table to perform amputations. The wounded were taken to the shelter of the building's solid cellars. Although the Panzerschützen of SS-Panzer-Regiment 1 wore leather submarine clothing, burns were the main cause of serious injuries.[33] Jeanne Masson, a young teenager and the daughter of the tenant farmer, who was housed in the cellars, recalled: '*In an adjoining cellar there were wounded people who were all burned, I went to visit them. I was very impressed by their burns, their faces were very swollen like a sponge with holes in it, their mouths were welded shut, it was awful to see in addition to the repulsive smell and the groans of suffering...*'[34]

The second tank involved has not been identified, but it could be Panther 223 of Unterscharführer Kurt Baier. As soon as the fighting was over, this tank was taken to the foot of the Remouchamps quarries to serve as a target for the 57-mm anti-tank guns of the 504th Parachute Infantry Regiment (504th PIR) which was resting in the locality.[35]

Panther 211/212 with Stahlrollen is seen here being examined by US officers at Stoumont station. (*NARA*)

In order to tow the heavy armour easily, mechanics dismantled its tracks in front of Stoumont railway station. While it is very likely that the carcass of the big beast was close to the station, it appears that the second tank hit by Leon Kent's 90-mm gun was 250 metres from where the tracks were removed.[36] It could therefore have been another tank rather than the 223. The mystery remains.

At Halte de Lorcé, Colonel Sutherland's HQ, it was 11:00. General Hobbs had kept his promise, having lobbied V Corps HQ and obtained the 740th TB. The S2 of the regiment,[37] Captain Stonecipher, went in search of the armoured unit that was supposed to save them.

A Very Special Battalion

The 740th Tank Battalion (TB) was a special unit equipped with searchlights designed to illuminate the battlefield at night. It was equipped with CDL (Canal Defense Light) tanks using a powerful carbon arc searchlight mounted in a special turret. It was intended

A Sherman M4A3 76(w) was recommissioned by the 740th TB to defend the Amblève valley. (*Rights reserved via Legros Collard*)

for use in night attacks, when the light could target and dazzle enemy positions with a 13 million Candela searchlight and a machine gun.

The unit joined the First US Army in November 1944, without any equipment. As soon as he arrived, Lieutenant Colonel Rubel learned that his secret mission was cancelled and that his battalion was reconfigured to normal standards. This meant that he had to re-equip his unit with M4 Sherman tanks and M5A1 Stuart light tanks. Unfortunately, the FUSA could only equip the 740th TB with nine Shermans and a few M5s to familiarise themselves with their new mission. Headquarters promised that a full set of tanks might arrive in January. In the meantime, Rubel was ordered to make do. On 16 December, the battalion was in Neufchâteau, 80 kilometres from the front lines. Lieutenant Colonel Rubel remembers:

> *At 12:45 on 18 December, we received a phone call from Lieutenant Colonel Cox, FUSA deputy armour officer, indicating that things were going badly and getting worse fast. He said that the General wanted us to send a reinforced company to protect the installations in the vicinity of Aywaille, and to equip ourselves in a depot in Sprimont, a nearby town. The heavy vehicle depots were located in a quarry.*
>
> *I alerted the Battalion and ordered C Coy to take the lead. Captain Berry set off quickly, the men being without vehicles, they moved with the trucks of the service company. On arrival at Aywaille I reported to Colonel Lynde, the FUSA's orderly officer, who was*

The new M24 light tanks were unknown to American troops. Before their mass deployment, a few examples were presented to the soldiers. These demonstration vehicles were integrated into the ranks of the 740th TB. (*NARA*)

> *responsible for the defence of the depot. We had to equip ourselves as quickly as possible and take up a defensive position at Remouchamps.*
>
> *When I arrived at the depot I was frightened, only three Shermans were in working order. Out of about twenty-five tanks in the park, only fifteen could be made operational. Even these had been cannibalised to some extent. Generators and starters had been removed, engines, and other parts were missing. Weapons, radio transmitters and receivers were missing. Ammunition was also missing. We had a free hand, and we chose fifteen tanks that looked repairable. We worked all night cannibalising parts to make as many vehicles as possible operational. Very few of these vehicles had radios and the section leaders found it necessary to use visual signals. We discovered two new types of light tanks that had arrived at the depot by mistake, M24 Chaffees intended to replace the M5 Stuart. By noon on the 19th Captain Berry was in action at Remouchamps with two sections of five Shermans, and an M36 Jackson Tank Destroyer.*[38]

As soon as the 119th IR could dispose of the 740th TB, Captain Stonecipher, S2 of the regiment, went to Remouchamps to meet Captain Berry and convince him to intervene quickly, as the situation on the front was dramatic.

The Light Tank M5A1 of the 743rd TB arrived later and was sent to hunt down KG Von der Heydte. (*NARA*)

An M31 Armored Recorvery Vehicle on a Lee chassis is used to repair the tanks of the 740th TB. (*Rights reserved, Legros Collard*)

Lieutenant Colonel Rubel continues his account:

> *I arrived a few minutes after their meeting. Captain Berry told me about his conversation with the S2 while I was talking with him, Captain Stonecipher came back and pleaded to have the tanks. I told him that our orders were to stay where we were and that if any changes were to be made they should be made by higher authority. At 14:00 hours he returned, bringing General Hobbs who told me that he had spoken to General Hodges, Commander FUSA and obtained permission to attach the 740th Battalion to 30th ID. He ordered us to move immediately with all we could muster to help out of the critical situation. I asked Captain Berry to move out immediately and I followed Captain Stonecipher to the regimental headquarters.*

Contrary to the legend that Rubel would fabricate, it was not his unit that would stop Peiper's final attack, as he was re-equipping himself as the Panthers presented themselves for their second assault.

The 119th IR's Surge

Colonel Sutherland, at the head of the 119th IR, reacted with coolness to the fall of Stoumont and the rout of his III/119th IR. He established a powerful roadblock 1 kilometre from his headquarters, while his 1st Battalion took up position in a steep and

The scene of the confrontation on the outskirts of Stoumont station. (*Rights reserved*)

heavily wooded area. Two 90-mm anti-aircraft guns, placed in anti-tank mode, reinforced his last chance position, one belonging to the 143rd AAA Gun Battalion, the other to the 110th AAA Gun Battalion.[39] An M10 Tank Destroyer, the A-2[40] of the 823rd TDB, was on the defensive,[41] as well as Shermans of the 743rd TB. The second 90-mm gun of the 110th AAA Gun Battalion was positioned 500 metres back, just in front of Halte de Lorcé, at the level of a wood depot.

Although it had been slowed down around 12:00, the German attack soon resumed in full swing. The Sherman C-10[42] had the thankless role of slowing down the enemy charge, and was in the front line at the roadblock. On the German side, five Panthers were still intact and continued to push forward with the 11. SS-Pz-Gren-Rgt 2 accompanied by the Fallschirmjäger. While the infantry tried to bypass the roadblock through the forest section, Unterscharführer Krüger's Panther 215 drove at the head of the pack. Fifty metres before the last bend in the road leading to the new front line, the leading Panther entered the line of fire of the Sherman C-10, which fired and disabled Krüger's tank. Panther 215 remained stationary on the left side of the road, but did not catch fire. The killing of the beast is recorded in the 119th IR diary at 13:00. The driver of Panther 215, Oskar Guttmann, was wounded and transported to the field hospital based at the Château de Froidcour.

The enemy withdrew, but continued to fire intermittently.[43] The German infantry did not do any better, being stopped in their advance through the forest where they also withdrew with heavy losses. At about 15:30, Captain Berry of the 740th TB arrived. In addition to his half-cannibalised Shermans, his M5 and M24 light tanks, his team included an M-36 Jackson tank fighter armed with the dreaded 90-mm. The joint assault by these tanks and the infantry was scheduled for 16:00 at nightfall.

A Tissue of Lies

The first historians who worked on the story of KG Peiper used the sources at their disposal. In particular the book *Daredevil: The Story of the 740th Tank Battalion* written by the commander of the 740th TB, George K. Rubel. He tells the story in a very different way:

> *Captain Berry, the company commander, arrived at 15:30. We told him the situation. He was ordered to attack with the infantry. Lieutenant Powers was to lead the attack with his platoon, and Lieutenant Oglensky and his tanks were to follow him. We communicated to Lieutenant Colonel Hurlong, commander of the 1st Battalion, 119th IR that we would begin our attack at 16:00 hours.*
>
> *Lt Powers led the attack. He had only gone about 800 yards when he saw a Panther about 150 yards away on a bend in the road. His first shot hit the gun's mantle, ricocheted down, killed the enemy driver and gunner. The shot set the tank on fire. A few metres further on, a second tank appeared. He fired, the shell hit the front plate of the tank and ricocheted. His gun jammed and he signalled to Sergeant Loopey to take over quickly with his Tank Destroyer. The first round from his 90-mm gun set the tank on fire but he threw in a couple more rounds for good measure.*
>
> *By this time Lieutenant Powers had got the gun back into action and resumed his advance. About 150 yards further on he came upon the third Panther. His first shell blew*

The interior of a Sherman turret. (*NARA*)

the muzzle brake off the Panzer, and two more rounds set the tank on fire. The action took place in less than thirty minutes.

As soon as the attack began, a fine drizzle fell, and a blanket-like fog covered the whole area. It was difficult to see an object from 400 metres away. Lt Power's platoon had not only knocked out three tanks, his machine guns had sprayed the roadsides and hillsides and a number of the enemy were killed. Our success in thirty minutes of fighting was due to the Doughboys of the 119th. They had stopped giving ground, and joined in the attack, recovered more than the thousand yards of ground they had lost during the day.[44]

Such a version of events is surely worthy of the best Hollywood script! In the absence of other sources, which were classified as secret until the 1980s, there was no reason for early historians to question Rubel's account. John Toland, who paved the way for all of them, takes the story as it is.[45] Today, with new sources available, we know that this story is a tissue of lies. We are not the first to write it, but we are pleased to be able to confirm the work of other historians through different sources.[46]

The worst thing is that Lieutenant Colonel Rubel added:

I had never been so anxious in my life. I was apprehensive about sending my boys into battle with no experience. My fears were redoubled when I saw that the 743rd TB was withdrawing on the grounds that they were short of ammunition. They had received more ammunition than we had. He just did not have the guts. [...] Neither Captain Berry nor any of his men showed that they were nervous. The co-operation between the Battalion and the 119th IR was perfect.[47]

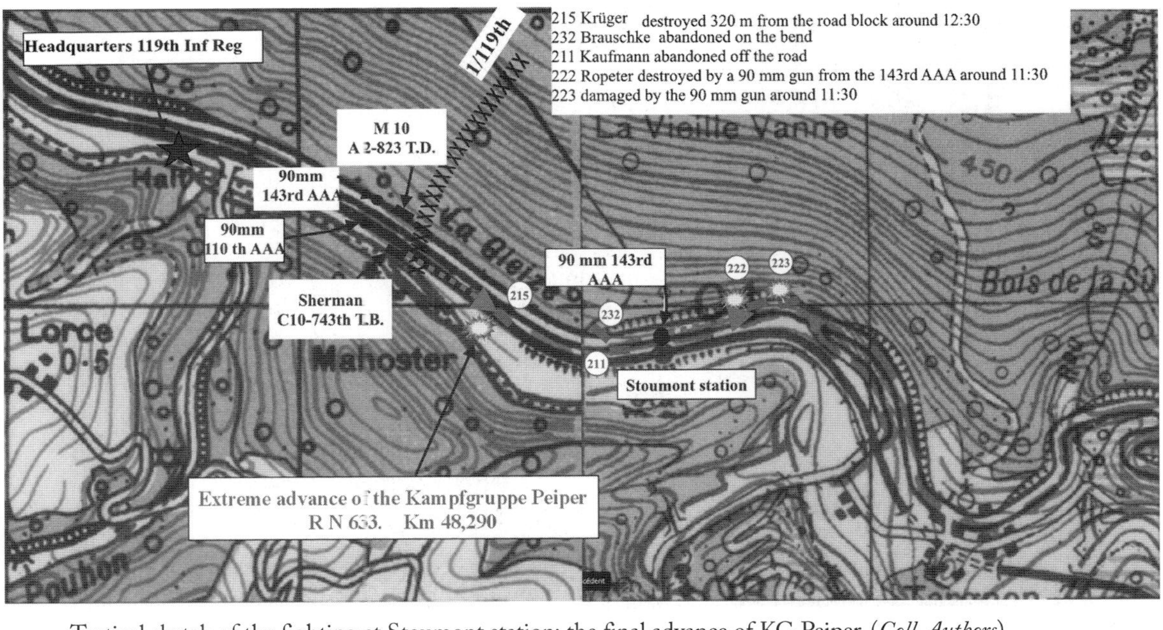

Tactical sketch of the fighting at Stoumont station; the final advance of KG Peiper. (*Coll. Authors*)

Attention to detail is needed here, and at a first glance, Rubel's testimony puts us immediately on the alert. The first Panther to be put out of action was undoubtedly Panther 215, the most advanced element of the Kamfpgruppe's armoured *Spitze*. The facts are clear: it was stopped by the supposed fire of the Sherman C10 of the 743rd TB, or of one of the 90-mm guns or even of the 3-inch gun equipping the Tank Destroyer M-10 A2. The killing of the beast is confirmed by two reports at about 12:00.[48] It is clear that Lieutenant Powers fired and hit Krüger's Panzer, but it was abandoned during the assault at 16:30. Concerning Unterscharführer Herbert Brauschke's Panther 232, the study of a photograph taken from a US film shot directly after the fighting (sadly unpublishable because of its poor quality[49]) allows us to see Panther 211 in the foreground and in the bend in the road Brauschke's Panther 232. It is clearly visible that the driver of 232 has thrown his tank into the ditch, although the exact reason as to why is unknown. It can be assumed that the driver voluntarily left the road so as not to block the passage of the other Panzers. It should be noted that these tanks had travelled more than 100 kilometres since they disembarked from the train that was supposed to bring them as close as possible to the front line.[50] Knowing that the mechanics of the Panther was calculated for armoured vehicles of 35 tonnes,[51] it displays more than 43 tonnes on the scale, meaning the German beast was certainly affected by excess weight, the cause of its comorbidity, and thus resulting in many failures. A fuel failure or a broken track are also possibilities. This second Panther was also abandoned during the loading of the 740th TB.

The third trophy claimed by Rubel was Panther 211 (formerly 212). In a photograph also taken from the US film,[52] the tank is shown with its muzzle brake intact while Powers claims to have hit it on the first shot. The destruction of the gun tip was therefore 'post mortem'. The MG 34 machine gun is missing, and its dismantling would have been

The underbody of this Panther was pierced by a mine, causing it to fall into a ditch. (*Rights reserved*)

Panther 215 was the tank of the Peiper column that reached the furthest into the US lines. Stopped at Stoumont station, it ended up on its back in a ditch. (*Rights reserved*)

carried out in a calm manner, which was never the case when a tank was mortally hit. In the following picture, Panther 232 can be seen on the left, turned over in the ditch. Panther 211 is out of the road, neither in an attack nor an ambush position, the 7.5-cm gun in the axis of the tank and not directed towards a potential enemy. During the assault by Captain Berry's tanks, the lead Sherman, that of Lieutenant Powers, had to get around the abandoned Panther 215. The distance between Powers' Sherman and Kaufmann's Panther 211 was 150 metres, so if the Panzer crew was in place, it is obvious that not even the worst gunner could miss such a target. At this distance, the terrible 7.5-cm gun forged by Rheinmetall was able to destroy any Allied armour.

The conclusion must therefore be that this Panther was also hit by fire after it had been abandoned. That is not to say that the American tankers lied, after all, in the stress of the action they certainly did not realise that the three Panzers were inert and harmless. They nevertheless courageously charged towards armoured vehicles that were much tougher than their own tanks.

Unsecured Flanks

After his failure in front of the Targnon station, Peiper could no longer push forward without receiving reinforcements and fuel. His lines of communication were under enemy fire. Only a weak umbilical cord remained. To reach it, the tail of the 1. SS-Panzer-Division, KG Knittel and KG Hansen, had to cross the Amblève on the Petit Spay bridge or take over the Stavelot bridge. Without securing its lines of communication, KG Peiper could not deepen its breakthrough. It was forced to gather at La Gleize for the night and hope that in its rear, things will turn out in its favour.

Conclusion

The Impossible Blitzkrieg

A Summary of the Facts

On the evening of 17 December, the Stab of the 6. Panzer-Armee still believed in a possible breakthrough in the sector, mainly due to lack of intelligence. In fact, the time lost during the first two days of the offensive had already doomed the success of the offensive in this sector. The reinforcements were on their way, but the halt on the heights of Stavelot gave the Americans the final respite they needed to pull themselves together.

On the morning of 18 December, the staff of the 6. Panzer-Armee could only note that things were already becoming complicated. The Volks-Grenadier-Divisionen of the LXVII. Armee-Korps were held in check. Their sector was heavily mined and as time went on, the American resistance was growing stronger. It became very clear that the objective of cutting the Eupen–Monschau and Eupen–Malmedy roads would not be achieved. Movement in the army's rear area was made very difficult by the destruction of the railway infrastructure. The schwere-Panzerjäger-Abteilung 653 and the schwere-

The beginning of the breakthrough was difficult for the Germans and there was no making up for lost time. (*NAC*)

The Panzer IV Ausf J like the one seen here fought alongside the Panthers and Tigers. The lack of homogeneity between the equipment would be a problem. (*NARA*)

Panzer-Abteilung 506 that were to be thrown into the fray did not arrive. The VGDs were clearly too weak and unorganised to achieve success. At the very least, the 6. Panzer-Armee would be satisfied if the American troops had remained fixed in this sector.

While the 82nd AbnD was on its way, KG Peiper continued its progression towards the Meuse. It left Stavelot and went straight ahead to leave the Amblève valley. Without a glance in the direction of Spa, where the large fuel depot was located, it turned south-west, passing through the small town of Trois-Ponts at the confluence of two valleys, where the bridge over the Amblève jumped in extremis. The same applied to the bridge over the Lienne a few kilometres further on.

As KG Peiper progressed, the resistance of the opponent stiffened. The time gained by the GIs, with heavy losses, meant a greater delay to the point that on the 19th, its last chances to break through had faded away.

The Basics are No Longer There

A successful Blitzkrieg required several prerequisites to work. First of all, it was necessary to be able to surprise the opponent. This surprise was undeniably present in the Ardennes, the numbers gathered by the German army completely surprising the SHAEF by their size. The time of year chosen allowed the Allied air force to be grounded. The latter was practically incapable of acting to support the troops on the ground; on the other

The smaller Sherman was more suitable for the Ardennes sector than the heavy Tiger. (*NARA*)

hand, the Luftwaffe was also largely absent. The cancellation of a disadvantage does not necessarily correspond to an advantage, however. The impact of the lack of air superiority was simply cancelled out during the first days of the *Wacht am Rhein* offensive. The third requirement was to assemble a strike force that was superior to the opponent at the point of attack. This condition was certainly met, but was partly to the attacker's disadvantage. The roads were so bad that the concentration of troops in quantities too large to be projected into battle generated monster traffic jams, caused in part by the resistance of the GIs in the front line. The day of the attack, 16 December, went badly for the Germans, who were confronted with restive troops along virtually the entire length of their front. The fact that the US position was practically dislocated the next day did not change anything; in war, lost time is never made up for. The day gained was enough to send the first reinforcements to the Ardennes and gradually cancel the numerical differential. The poor quality of the chosen roads also slowed down the exploitation of the breakthrough, giving the defenders even more time to react.

By 19 December, only the third day of the German onslaught, American troops had more than doubled on the Ardennes front. There were already three armoured divisions in the battle. A fourth, the 3rd Armored Division, was about to arrive in the front line, and ten infantry divisions, including two airborne divisions, were now facing the German troops.[1]

Flying Without Regard to its Flanks

Deprived of reinforcements and supplies, Peiper did not immediately realise the seriousness of his situation and continued to try to make his way towards the Meuse. When his fuel ran out, he was forced to take up a defensive position on the heights of La

Gleize. There, he was hammered all day long and saw his firepower eroded little by little. He eventually had to scuttle his precious tanks, mainly Panthers and Tigers, to reach his lines on foot. This American victory was first won in the streets of Stavelot on 18 and 19 December.

Thinking only of reaching the Meuse as quickly as possible, Peiper rushed forward without dispatching elements of his column to secure his lines of communication. This lack of caution was fatal as the GIs took back the city free of enemy troops and cut off the SS division's armoured fist from all supplies. Surrounded in the Stoumont-La Gleize cauldron, the most powerful German battle group of the Battle of the Bulge ran out of fuel. It was the first to be neutralised by the Allies. Only about 800 men escaped and managed to reach their lines, abandoning their powerful weapons. Logistics is the key to the success or failure of any military operation, making it undoubtedly the queen of any battle.

American Genius

What saved the American front in the sector in particular was the initiative shown by the 1111th Engineer Combat Group. The four major facts that really delayed Peiper were linked to the activities of the US combat engineer units. Firstly, there were the mines and the destruction of bridges in the initial attack. Then the blockade on the Stavelot heights caused Peiper to postpone his assault until the following day. The bridge over the Amblève at Trois-Pont forced him to change his route, otherwise he would have caught the 82nd AbnD in the middle of the transfer. Finally, the bridge over the River Lienne was destroyed, thus protecting the paratroopers' deployment. Without the crucial action of the sappers, the battle could have taken a completely different turn!

The Importance of Operational Tempo

To win in a mechanised war, you have to set the tempo for your opponent. The belligerent who wants to conduct a real Blitzkrieg must, above all, acquire the means to keep the initiative throughout the campaign. To do this, it must give such a high rhythm to its operations that its enemy is unable to have time to analyse the blows dealt to it and choose an appropriate reaction. The speed differential must be such that the orders given by the opponent are already out of date by the time they reach the units at the front. This is not just a matter of applying what strategists call the principle of initiative, which '*commands us not to wait for the enemy's action, but to anticipate him in such a way as to deprive him of his freedom of action and to force him to undergo our will,*'[2] but to go even further. Indeed, during a Blitzkrieg, the advantage is kept by systematically acting faster than the opponent. It is this specificity that is at the origin of the adjective that describes this way of conducting operations.[3]

In 1944, it was no longer the French armoured divisions that had to be fought, but the modernity of the US army, every infantry division of which was motorised. In this final

The lines of communication were the Achilles' heel of the German attack. (*NAC*)

phase of the conflict, similar units of the Wehrmacht were still largely horse-drawn. The temporal analysis of the course of events in the sector of the 6. Panzer-Armee highlights the unfavourable evolution of the Panzer-Divisionen. The surprise attack was launched at dawn on 16 December 1944. The next morning, Eisenhower was aware of the scale of the German operations and made the right operational decisions, all within barely 24 hours. He dispatched the 7th Armored Division to the St. Vith sector and other units followed quickly. The reaction time of the US armoured divisions was thus equivalent to that of the large German armoured units.

Moreover, on the ground, Peiper was unable to impose his tempo on his opponent. The breakthrough achieved at great cost on the evening of 16 December was barely exploited on the 17th: Stavelot did not fall into his hands. It was already almost too late to achieve a lightning breakthrough.

Appendix

Equivalent Military Ranks

The Waffen-SS had their own rank designations, which in turn were different to those of the Wehrmacht [army]. To help readers understand, the following table shows the SS equivalent ranks in the American and British armies.

Waffen-SS	*British Army*	*US Army*
…….	*Field Marshal*	*General of the Army*
Oberstgruppenführer	*General*	*General*
Obergruppenführer	*Lieutenant General*	*Lieutenant General*
Gruppenführer	*Major General*	*Major General*
Brigadeführer	*Brigadier*	*Brigadier General*
Oberführer	*Colonel (Senior)*	*Colonel (Senior)*
Standartenführer	*Colonel*	*Colonel*
Obersturmbannführer	*Lieutenant Colonel*	*Lieutenant Colonel*
Sturmbannführer	*Major*	*Major*
Hauptsturmführer	*Captain*	*Captain*
Obersturmführer	*Lieutenant*	*First Lieutenant*
Untersturmführer	*Second Lieutenant*	*Second Lieutenant*
Sturmscharführer	*Regimental Sergeant Major*	*Sergeant Major*
Stabsscharführer	*Sergeant Major*	…….
Hauptscharführer	*Sergeant Major*	*Master Sergeant*
Oberscharführer	*Staff Sergeant*	*Technical Sergeant*
Scharführer	*Sergeant*	*Staff Sergeant*
Unterscharführer	*Corporal*	*Sergeant*
Rottenführer (Squad Leader)	*Lance Corporal*	*Corporal*
Sturmmann (Storm Trooper)	*Senior Private*	*Private First Class*
Oberschütze	…….	*Senior Private*
Schütze	*Private*	*Private*

Notes

Chapter 1

1. Hasso Eccard von Manteuffel (1897-1978) was General der Panzertruppen at the time of the Battle of the Bulge. He commanded the 5. Panzer-Armee as it attacked in the Bastogne Dinant sector.
2. 'The only salvation for the defeated is to hope for no salvation'.
3. Warlimont, W., *5 ans au GQG de Hitler*, Paris, 1975, pp.295-7.
4. The Supreme Command of the Wehrmacht (OKW), together with the Supreme Command of the Army (OKH), the Supreme Command of the Navy (OKM) and the Supreme Command of the Air Force (OKL), was one of the highest staff organisations of the German army. The OKW and the High Commands of the three branches of the armed forces assumed planning tasks in their respective areas of responsibility. They were subordinate to the Supreme Commander of the Wehrmacht, Adolf Hitler.
5. Washington, NARA, ETHINT 50, p.8.
6. Blümentritt, G., *Von Rundstedt: The Soldier and the Man*, London, 1952, p.265.
7. The Big Solution.
8. Quoted in Blümentritt, G., *Von Rundstedt: The Soldier and the Man*, London, 1952, p.268.
9. Fort Leaveworth, Ike Skelton Library, N17500-1033-2, MSB 151, p.25.
10. The 6. Panzer-Armee was not yet called the SS-Panzer-Armee as it also covered units of the Wehrmacht.
11. Washington, NARA, ETHINT 45, pp.2-3.
12. Liddell Hart, B.H., *Les généraux allemands parlent,* Paris, 1949, p.298.
13. Ibid, pp.297-9.
14. Washington, NARA, ETHINT 21, p.2.
15. Washington, NARA, ETHINT 50, p.9.
16. Washington, NARA, ETHINT 45, p.4.
17. The Ia (pronounced Einz A) was the chief of staff of a given unit.
18. Logistics officer.
19. Washington, NARA, ETHINT 21, p.3.
20. Liddell Hart, B.H., *Les généraux allemands parlent,* Paris, 1949, p.301.
21. Fort Leaveworth, Ike Skelton Library, N17500-1033-2, MSB 151, passim.
22. Liddell Hart, B.H., *Les généraux allemands parlent,* Paris, 1949, p.304.
23. Washington, NARA, ETHINT 45, p.3.
24. Washington, NARA, ETHINT 50, p.14.

Chapter 2

1. Supreme Headquarters Allied Expeditionary Force, the headquarters of the Allied forces in North-Western Europe.
2. Or combat squadron.
3. Tactical aviation, the term for a ground attack squadron.
4. See: Wenkin, H., *De la terreur à la Lune*, Paris-Neufchâteau, 2020, pp.177-82.
5. Speer, A., *At the Heart of the Third Reich*, Paris, 1971, p.569.
6. Liddell Hart, B.H., *Les généraux allemands parlent,* Paris, 1949, pp.300-301.

7. Washington, NARA, Ethint 21, p.4.
8. Washington, NARA, Ethint 10, p.8.

Chapter 3

1. Washington, Center of Military History, Logistics in World War II Final Report of the Army Forces, p.159.
2. Washington Center of Military History, The European Theater of Operations LOGISTICAL SUPPORT OF THE ARMIES, Vol I, pp.412-13.
3. Carlisle Barracks Pennsylvania, US Army College, USAWC Strategy research project from the Red Ball Express, pp.6-7.
4. Fort Leavenworth, Ike Skelton Library, Sustainment improvisation - Expanding the realm of the possible, p.22.
5. Washington Center of Military History, The European Theater of Operations LOGISTICAL SUPPORT OF THE ARMIES, Vol II, p.148.
6. Washington, DC, NARA, Administrative History Collection, G4 History, ADM No. 553, December 1944 - January 1945, p.5.
7. American-British-Canadian for some and Antwerp-Brussels-Charleroi for others.
8. Washington, NARA, Administrative History Collection, G4 History, ADM No. 553, December 1944 - January 1945, p.21.
9. Without distinction between divisions, whether infantry, armoured, at rest or on the front line.
10. Washington Center of Military History, The European Theater of Operations LOGISTICAL SUPPORT OF THE ARMIES, Vol II, pp.170-4.
11. Heptia, T., *Historique de la base de Bierset,* Bierset, 1990, p.87.
12. Washington Center of Military History, The European Theater of Operations LOGISTICAL SUPPORT OF THE ARMIES, Vol II, p.168.
13. Ibid. p.207.
14. Washington, NARA, HEADQUARTERS 12TH ARMY GROUP (FINAL AFTER ACTION REPORT), Vol II, p.22.
15. Ibid, p.208.
16. Ibid, p.183.
17. The place where the jerry cans were located was actually on the old road, the new one is 2 kilometres away.

Chapter 4

1. The one that had been destroyed at Stalingrad and reconstituted to continue the fight on the Eastern Front.
2. Washington, NARA, ETHINT 15, p.1.
3. Rockenbrod, F., *L'inutile calvaire de la Panzer-Abteilung 506* in Wenkin, H. (ed.), *Patton mis au pas, Mook, 1944 No. 5*, Neufchâteau, 2020, p.119.
4. Freiburg, Bundesarchiv, MSA 924, Kraemer, F., *Einsatz der 6. Panzer-Armee in den Ardennen,* report of October 1945, pp.1-16.
5. Washington, NARA, ETHINT 15, p.2.
6. Washington, NARA, ETHINT 15, p.5.
7. The order specifies '*Ohne Rücksicht auf ihre Flanken*', without a backward glance at its flanks.
8. Washington, NARA ETHINT 25, Interview with Fritz Kraemer concerning the use of the LXVII AK from 16 to 26 December 1944, dated 17 November 1945.
9. Freiburg, Bundesarchiv, MSA 924, Kraemer, F., *Einsatz der 6. Panzer-Armee in den Ardennen,* report of October 1945, pp.1-14.
10. Washington, NARA, ENTHINT 23, Interview with Fritz Kraemer concerning the 6. Panzer-Armee from 16 to 19 December 1944, dated 12 July 1949.
11. Washington, NARA, MSB 347, Staudinger, W., *The artillery command of the 6th Panzer Army during the Ardennes Offensive, 1944-1945,* report of January 1951, annex 1.

12. Götzel, H., *Generaloberst Kurt Student und seine Fallschirmjäger, die Erinnerungen des Generaloberst Kurt Student*, Friedberg, s.d., [1980], p.495.
13. Freiburg, Bundesarchiv, MSA 877, Priess, H., *Einsatz des I SS Pz Korps waehrend der den Ardennen-Offensive Dezember 1944 Januar 1945,* report of March 1946, pp.9-19.
14. In German, the noun Gruppe (group) is feminine, so we respect the gender. *Kampfgruppe* simply means fighting group.
15. Reynolds, M., *The Devil's Warrant Officer*, Erpe, 2000, pp.37-8.
16. Washington, NARA, ETHINT 10, Interview with Obst Joachim Peiper, 1. SS-Panzer-Regiment (11-24 Dec 1944), interview of 7 September 1945, pp.1-2.

Chapter 5

1. The *Notek* was a night light that allowed a driver to navigate in the dark without the vehicle being detected by a ground observer or aircraft.
2. Tiemann, R., *The Leibstandarte Vol IV part 2*, Winnipeg, 1998, p.27.
3. Washington, NARA ETHINT 10, Interview with Obst Joachim Peiper, 1. SS-Panzer-Regiment (11-24 Dec 1944), interview of 7 September 1945, pp.2-4.
4. The instruction does not speak of a Kampfgruppe, but of an armoured group Gepanzerte Gruppe.
5. Tiemann, R., *The Leibstandarte Vol IV part 2*, Winnipeg, 1998, p.25.
6. The Ombret-Rausa crossing point.
7. Washington, NARA, ETHINT 10, Interview with Obst Joachim Peiper, 1. SS-Panzer-Regiment (11-24 Dec 1944), interview of 7 September 1945, p.7.
8. Peiper used this term to describe the Eifel heights.
9. Washington, NARA, ETHINT 10, Interview with Obst Joachim Peiper, 1. SS-Panzer-Regiment (11-24 Dec 1944), interview of 7 September 1945, p.9.
10. A Zug was a tank platoon. Its size varied as the conflict progressed.
11. Cooke, D. and Evans, W., *Kampfgruppe Peiper at the Battle of the Bulge,* Mechanicsburgs, 2005, p.27.

Chapter 6

1. Washington, NARA, MSB 733, 12th Volks Grenadier Division (3-29 December 1944), report by Generalleutnant Gerhard Engel, dated 27 December 1947, pp.1-4.
2. Wijers, H., *The Battle of the Bulge: The Losheim Gap/Holding the Line*, Mechanicsburg, 2009, pp.27-6.
3. Washington, NARA, MSB 733, 12th Volks Grenadier Division (3-29 December 1944), report by Generalleutnant Gerhard Engel, dated 27 December 1947, pp.4-5.
4. Wijers, H., *The Battle of the Bulge: The Losheim Gap/Holding the Line*, Mechanicsburg, 2009, p.43.
5. Washington, NARA, ETHINT 10, Interview with Obst Joachim Peiper, 1. SS-Panzer-Regiment (11-24 Dec 1944), interview of 7 September 1945, p.14.
6. Cooke, D. and Evans, W., *Kampfgruppe Peiper at the Battle of the Bulge,* Mechanicsburgs, 2005, p.35.
7. Washington, NARA, ETHINT 10, p.15.
8. Rest Centre.
9. Washington, NARA, RG407/427A/ box 19014/ folder CI 329A-14 / combat interview A Troop, p.5.
10. https://www.grenzecho.net/art/zz/reportagen/besuch-von-marlene-dietrich-in-honsfeld-in-letzter-minute-abgesagt-, consulted on 7 December 2022. On 14 December the actress was performing in Bastogne before Middleton, the next day she was in Wiltz before the 28th ID, on the 16th she was in Honsfeld.
11. In reality the 394th IR.
12. Frühbeisser, R., *Opfergang deutscher Fallschirmjäger*, s.l., 1966, p.243.
13. Washington, NARA, RG407/427A/ box 19014/ folder CI 329A-14/ combat interview A Troop, pp.5-6.

14. Frühbeisser, R., *Opfergang deutscher Fallschirmjäger*, s.l., 1966, pp.243-4.
15. Feldwebel (nurse) Otto died on 19 December 1944 in the military hospital as a result of a shrapnel wound to the heart.
16. Frühbeisser, R., *Opfergang deutscher Fallschirmjäger*, s.l., 1966, pp.245-6.
17. A formation belonging to the 2nd Infantry Division.
18. Fort Leavenworth, Ike Skelton Library, 847-9, AAR 612th TDB, entry of 18 December 1944.
19. Washington, NARA, RG407/427A/ box 19014/ folder CI 329A-14/ combat interview A Troop, pp.7-8.
20. Washington, NARA, RG407/427A/ box 19014/ folder CI 329B-14/ After Action Report of the 14th Cavalry Group, entry 17 February 1944.
21. Frühbeisser, R., *Opfergang deutscher Fallschirmjäger*, s.l., 1966, pp.247-8.
22. Washington, NARA, ETHINT 10, p.15.
23. Frühbeisser, R., *Opfergang deutscher Fallschirmjäger*, s.l., 1966, pp.145 and 255.
24. Washington, NARA, ETHINT 11, p. 2.
25. Washington, NARA, ETHINT 10, p.17.

Chapter 7

1. Washington, NARA, ETHINT 10, p.17.
2. Rogister, H., *Décembre 1944 Bataille des Ardennes De Baugner à Stavelot,* CRIBA, Liège, 2009, p.31.
3. Ibid.
4. Rogister, H., *Décembre 1944 Bataille des Ardennes De Baugner à Stavelot,* CRIBA, Liège, 2009, p.39.
5. Longue, M., *Massacres en Ardennes*, Brussels, 2006, pp.150-3.
6. Testimony of Joachim Peiper, quoted in Thompson, R.L., *The ETO Ardennes Campaign of the Combat Group Peiper 16-26 December 1944*, p.36.
7. Rogister, H., *Décembre 1944 Bataille des Ardennes De Baugner à Stavelot,* CRIBA, Liège, 2009, p.38.
8. Testimony of Hermann Priess, quoted in Thompson, R.L., *The ETO Ardennes Campaign of the Combat Group Peiper 16-26 December 1944*, p.33.
9. Ibid, p.36.
10. Rogister, H., *Décembre 1944 Bataille des Ardennes De Baugner à Stavelot,* CRIBA, Liège, 2009, p.7.
11. Testimony of Josef Dietrich, quoted in Thompson, R.L., *The ETO Ardennes Campaign of the Combat Group Peiper 16-26 December 1944*, p.30.
12. Rogister, H., *Décembre 1944 Bataille des Ardennes De Baugner à Stavelot,* CRIBA, Liège, 2009, p.7.
13. The text of the testimony, translated into English, uses the term reckless.
14. Longue, M., *Massacres en Ardennes*, Brussels, 2006, p.241.
15. Testimony of Joachim Peiper, quoted in Thompson, R.L., *The ETO Ardennes Campaign of the Combat Group Peiper 16-26 December 1944*, p.35.
16. Washington, NARA, ETHINT 10, p.9.
17. Rogister, H., *Décembre 1944 Bataille des Ardennes De Baugner à Stavelot,* CRIBA, Liège, 2009, p.10.
18. Brussels, Archives of the College of Procurators General, Trial of Stavelot Goltz and others. Translation of the written statement of Manfred Goblenz of 15 April 1946 in Schwäbisch Hall, Germany.
19. Quoted in Longue, M., *Massacres en Ardennes*, Brussels, 2006, p.61.
20. Quoted in Longue, M., *Massacres en Ardennes*, Brussels, 2006, p.57.
21. Fort Leaven Worth, Ike Skelton Library, N-17840, War Experiences of Commanders of German Panzer Units, General Sepp Dietrich and Colonel Joachim Peiper.
22. Washington, NARA, MSC-24, pp.90-1.
23. Evere, SGRS SA, Box AS, folder 181, staff note of 25 September 1944.
24. Meyer, K., *Soldier of the Reich*, Bayeux, 1996, p.410.
25. Longue, M., *Massacres en Ardennes*, Brussels, 2006, p.141.
26. War Crimes Commission, *Stavelot,* Liège, 1945, passim.
27. Longue, M., *Massacres en Ardennes*, Brussels, 2006, p.243.

Chapter 8

1. Washington NARA, ETHINT 10, interrogations of Peiper, dated 7 September 1944, p.18.
2. Armoured tip.
3. Rank in the Waffen-SS corresponding to that of lieutenant.
4. At this time Sternebeck was in Panther 625, as his own tank had been disabled by a mine at Büllingen.
5. The Hôtel du Moulin, which still exists today.
6. Wijers, H., *Battle of the Bulge, Vol 2: Hell at Bütgenbach / Seize the Bridges*, Mechanicsburg, 2010, p.164.
7. Reynolds, M., *The Devil's Adjutant*, Stapelhurst, 2002, p.99.
8. The first reconnaissance battalion of the SS.
9. An M8 Armored Car Greyhound, six-wheeled vehicle, armed with a 37-mm gun.
10. Operation placed under the responsibility of Otto Skorzeny, consisting, among other things of contingents disguised as American soldiers in charge of taking the bridges over the Meuse by surprise and creating disarray behind the American lines.
11. Wijers, H., *Battle of the Bulge, Vol 2: Hell at Bütgenbach / Seize the Bridges,* Mechanicsburg, 2010, pp.162-3.
12. Longue, M., *Massacres en Ardennes*, Brussels, 2006, pp.155-6.
13. Cain, F., *The 1111th Engineer Group in the Bulge: The Role of Engineers as Infantry in Airland Battle*, School of Advanced Military Studies US Army Command and General Staff College Fort Leavenworth, Kansas, 1985, pp.2-4.
14. Testimony of Charles Chuck Hensel quoted in Cuppens, G., *Massacre à Malmedy*, Bayeux, 1989, pp.48-50.
15. Ethint 10 interrogations of Peiper, dated 7 September 1944, pp.18-19.
16. Cuppens, G., *Massacre à Malmedy*, Bayeux, 1989, p.50.
17. Ibid. pp.19-20.
18. At that time the parade route was not as wide as it is today, so it was not possible to manoeuvre easily to negotiate turns.
19. Quoted in Cuppens, G., *Massacre à Malmedy*, Bayeux, 1989, p.41.

Chapter 9

1. Fort Leavenworth, Ike Skelton Library, AAR 825th TDB, entry of 18 December 1944.
2. Testimony of SS-Scharführer Rayer quoted in Reynolds, M., *The Devil's Adjudant*, Stapelhurst, 2002, p.120.
3. Washington, NARA, ETHINT 10, Interrogation of Peiper, dated 7 September 1944, p.20.
4. This is the fourth 3-inch gun, under the command of Sergeant Celentano, in position at the town kiosk.
5. 'Driver, let's go!'
6. 'Gunner, fire!'
7. 'Driver, speed up.'
8. Reynolds, M., *The Devil's Adjudant*, Stapelhurst, 2002, p.120.
9. The Panther Ausf G was equipped with a frontal armour invulnerable to the small gun, its side bottom was 40mm vertical. A thickness that could easily pierce the 57-mm, provided that one aimed well. It was necessary to place the shell between the higher part and the top of the tracks.
10. Report by US Army Historian Captain Ferris, Stavelot chapter. The officer wrote the document in January 1945 by interviewing the survivors. His report, which is intended to be precise and dramatic, gives only information that should be put into perspective.
11. Castor, H., *La route des massacres*, Erpe, 2005, pp.97-107.
12. SPW: abbreviation for Schützepanzerwagen, armoured semi-trailer.
13. Longue, M., *Kampfgruppe Knittel. L'odyssée de la SS-Aufklärungs-Abteilung 1 en terre ardennaise (16-27 December 1944)*, Damigny, 2010, pp.41 and 44.

14. Marcel Magain ended his military career with the rank of major general in the Air Force.
15. Pierre Suinen remained in the army after the war and ended his career as a major.
16. The Belgian soldiers were equipped and armed by the British.
17. Lauter, T., *December 18, 1944, Between Spa and Stavelot,* http://www.criba.be, Accessed 23 August 2019.
18. Laby, H., *Ardennes 44 Stavelot.* Faimes, 1999, pp.150-1.
19. Stairs, H., A cameo of history from the Battle of the Bulge, http://criba.be, Accessed 23 August 2018.
20. Stavelot Library, Stavelot 40/45, Stavelot, 1985, p.54.
21. Mocnik, J., 30 Hotitreurs of helle of Stavelot 17-18 December 1944, http://criba.be, Accessed 23 August 2018.
22. CFR supra.
23. Cain, F., *The 1111th Engineer Group in the Bulge: The Role of Engineers as Infantry in Airland Battle, Fort Leavenworth,* 1985, pp.10-13.
24. Cole, H., *La grande bataille des Ardennes en Belgique et au Luxembourg*, Villance-en-Ardennes, 1994, p.239.
25. Merriam, R., *Dark December,* New York-Chicago, 1947, p.162. The information is also taken up by Cole, who seems to have been inspired by Merriam's work to describe this engagement. Cain specifies that there were six .50s and four .30s.
26. Interview by Christian Dujardin with Mr Philippe Grégoire, son of the civilian convenience store owner.
27. Pergrin, D., *First Across the Rhine*, Saint-Paul, 2006, pp.143-4.
28 American time was one hour behind German time.
29 Gavin, J., *On to Berlin,* New York, 1978, p.215.
30 Interview by Christian Dujardin with Mr Philippe Grégoire.
31 Washington, NARA, ETHINT 11, Interview with Peiper by Lieutenant Tobin, 18 September 1945.
32 Washington, NARA, ETHINT 10, Interview with Peiper by Major Hechler, 7 September 1945.
33. Pergrin, D., *First Across the Rhine*, Saint Paul, 2006, p.144.
34. Freiburg, Bundesarchiv, MSA 924, Kraemer, F., *Einsatz der 6. Panzer-Armee in den Ardennen,* report of October 1945, pp.30-2.
35. Cailloux, L., *Ardennes 1944, Pearl Harbor in Europe*, First part, Liège, 1969, p.88.
36. Brussels, Royal Meteorological Institute, Spa Station.
37. Washington, NARA, ETHINT 10, Interview with Peiper by Major Hechler, 7 September 1945.

Chapter 10

1. Cable S71400 in Chandler, A. et al, eds, *The Papers of Dwight David Eisenhower*, Baltimore – London, Vol IV, 1971, pp.23–56.
2. Washington, NARA, After Action Report, Headquarters 30th Infantry-Division, entry dated 17 December 1944.
3. Martell, C., http://www.criba.be, Accessed on 25 March 2018.
4. Fort Leavenworth, Ike Skelton Library, 743rd Tank Battalion, S3 Journal-History November – December 1944, p.16.
5. Washington, NARA, ETHINT 21, p.5.
6. A commissioned officer after an exceptionally short training period of ninety days.
7. Thayer, K., *The Young Liberators*, Vol 2, Whitesboro, 2019, pp.49-50.
8. Ridgway, M., *Soldier: The Memoirs of Matthew B. Ridgway,* New York, 1956, pp.112-13.
9. Gavin, J., *On to Berlin,* New York, 1978, pp.203-204.
10. Fort Leavenworth, Ike Skelton Library, Adams, J., *The Operations of A Company, 508th PIR (82nd Airborne Division) near Rencheux, Belgium, 22-25 December 1944 (personal experience of a Company Commander)*, Fort Benning, 1947-1948, pp.3-4.
11. The S3 was the officer in charge of operations.

12. Fort Leavenworth, Ike Skelton Library, Campana, V., *The Operations of the 2nd Battalion, 504th PIR (82nd Airborne Division) in the German Counter Offensive 18 December 1944 – 16 January 1945 (personal experience of a Battalion S 3)*, Fort Benning, 1946-1947, p.5.
13. Fort Leavenworth, Ike Skelton Library, Marschall, S., *The Operations of 1st Platoon, Battery C, 80th Airborne Antiaircraft Battalion (82nd Airborne Division) in the Battle of the Bulge 17 December 1944 – 3 January 1945 (personal experience of a Platoon Leader)*, Fort Benning, 1947-1948, p.5.
14. Fort Leavenworth, Ike Skelton Library, Le Febvre, H., *The Operations of the 2nd Battalion, 508th PIR (82nd Airborne Division) in the Withdrawal and the Recapture of Thier du Mont Ridge, Belgium, 22 December 1944 – 7 January 1945 (personnal experience of a Battalion Operations Officer)*, Fort Benning, 1948-1949, p.5.
15. Adams, J., *The Operations of A Company, 508th PIR (82nd Airborne Division) near Rencheux, Belgium, 22-25 December 1944 (personal experience of a Company Commander)*, Fort Benning, 1947-1948, p.4.
16. Campana, C., *The Operations of the 2nd Battalion, 504th PIR (82nd Airborne Division) in the German Counter Offensive 18 December 1944 – 16 January 1945 (personal experience of a Battalion S 3)*, Fort Benning, 1946-1947, p.8.
17. Adams, J., *The Operations of A Company, 508th PIR (82nd Airborne Division) near Rencheux, Belgium, 22-25 December 1944 (personal experience of a Company Commander)*, Fort Benning, 1947-1948, p.4.
18. Ibid.
19. Campana, C., *The Operations of the 2nd Battalion, 504th PIR (82nd Airborne Division) in the German Counter Offensive 18 December 1944 – 16 January 1945 (personal experience of a Battalion S 3)*, Fort Benning, 1946-1947, p.9.
20. Gavin, J., *On to Berlin*, New York, 1978, pp.205-207.
21. This nickname was given to them by Axis Sally, AKA Mildred Gillars.
22. Thayer, K., *The Young Liberators*, Vol 2, Whitesboro, 2019, p.50.
23. Ibid.
24. Ibid.
25. Ibid, p.51.
26. Fort Leavenworth, Ike Skelton Library, No entry date, Journal 823rd Tanker Destroyer Battalion. Stoumont action.
27. Fort Leavenworth, Ike Skelton Library, AAR 823rd Tanker Destroyer Battalion, 19 December.
28. Washington, Library of Congress, Veterans History Project, Interview with Leon Kent, 20 July 2003.
29. Washington, NARA, Ferris, F., Historical Officer, 30th Infantry Division, 16-25 December 1944, p.31.
30. Hewitt R., *Workhorse of the Western Front*, Washington, 1946, p.176.
31. Fort Leavenworth, Ike Skelton Library, AAR 743rd Tank Batallion, November – December 1944.
32. Gavin, J., *On to Berlin*, New York, 1978, p.216.
33. Neufmoulin is a hamlet of a few houses on the banks of the Amblève, a few hundred metres from Habiémont. The bridge had been rebuilt in September by the 291st ECB.
34. Cain, F., *The 1111th Engineer Group in the Bulge: The Role of Engineers as Infantry in Airland Battle, Fort Leavenworth*, 1985, p.17.
35. Pergrin, D., *First Across the Rhine, The 291st Engineer Combat Battalion in France, Belgium and Germany*, St Paul, USA, 2006, p.131.
36. Gavin, J., *On to Berlin*, New York, 1978, p.217.

Chapter 11

1. NARA, Washington, MS C-04, p.9.
2. Analysis based on GSGS map no. 4040 of Malmedy (sheet 81), 1942 edition.
3. Pergrin, D., *First Across the Rhine*, Saint-Paul, 2006, p.133. Note that Peiper places the event two hours later.

4. Ibid, p.135.
5. Fort Leavenworth, Ike Skelton Library, AAR 823rd TD, entry of 18 December 1944.
6. Logbook of the 39th IR/30th ID, entry of 18th December 1944.
7. Burns, D., *Jump into the Valley of Shadow*, Haverton, 2011, p.192.
8. Marschall, S., *The Operations of 1st Platoon, Battery C, 80th Airborne Antiaircraft Battalion (82nd Airborne Division) in the Battle of the Bulge 17 December 1944 – 3 January 1945 (personal experience of a Platoon Leader)*, Fort Benning, 1947-1948, p.7.
9. Bundes Archiv, Freiburg, MS A-873, pp.9-10.
10. Ridgway, M., *Soldier: The Memoirs of Matthew B. Ridgway*, New York, 1956, p.115.
11. 8,426,000 litres.
12. Washington Center of Military History, The European Theater of Operations LOGISTICAL SUPPORT OF THE ARMIES, Vol II, p.183.
13. Fort Leavenworth, Ike Skelton Library, HEADQUARTERS 12TH ARMY GROUP (FINAL AFTER ACTION REPORT), VOL II, p.183.
14. Washington. NARA, ETHINT 10, p.8.
15. Ibid, p.16.
16. Brussels, Archives du Collège des Procureurs Généraux, Trial of Stavelot Goltz and others. Translation of the written statement of Manfred Goblenz of 15 April 1946 in Schwäbisch Hall, Germany.
17. Author's note: This was Kampfgruppe Peiper moving towards Cheneux.
18. Fort Leavenworth, Ike Skelton Library, Ferris, F., *The German Offensive 16 December Defense of Spa Gas Dump*, pp.1-5.
19. Author's note: This is a so-called Maxon Mount trailer with four 50 calibre Browning machine guns attached.
20. Speer, L., *110th AAA, Driving Hitler's Crawlin' Coffin*, Wroclaw, n. d., pp.195-7.
21. For more details on this subject, see the book dedicated to the *501. s SS-Pz-Abt* by the authors in the same collection.
22. Criba Fund, After Action Report, Headquarters 30th Infantry Division, entry of 18 December 1944.
23. Criba Fund, After Action Report, Headquarters 823rd TDB, entry of 18 December 1944.
24. Criba Fonds, After Action Report, Headquarters 30th Infantry Division, entry of 19 December 1944.
25. Freiburg, Bundesarchiv, MS-A 877, report by Priess, p.35.
26. Campana, C., *The Operations of the 2nd Battalion, 504th PIR (82nd Airborne Division) in the German Counter Offensive 18 December 1944 – 16 January 1945 (personal experience of a Battalion S 3)*, Fort Benning, 1946-1947, p.10.

Chapter 12

1. Author's note: 2. SS-Panzer-Regiment 1 signifies 2nd Panzer Company of the 1st Regiment.
2. De Meyer, S., Haasler, T., MacDougall, R., Vosters, S., Weber, H., *Duel in the Mist*, Newcastle, 2007, pp.14-15.
3. Hauptsturmführer, captain in the SS.
4. Aide de camp.
5. Major of the SS.
6. Lieutenant of the SS.
7. Company Commander.
8. Chief Warrant Officer of the SS.
9. Head of Section.
10. Second Lieutenant in the SS.
11. SS Warrant Officer.
12. Corporal of the SS.
13. III. (Gp.)/SS-Pz-Gren-Rgt 2 = 3rd (Transported) SS-Panzergrenadier (Infantry) Battalion of the 2nd Regiment.
14. 1. SS-Pz-Art-Rgt 1: 1st Company of the SS Panzer Artillery 1st Regiment.

15. 13. (IG)/SS-Pz-Gr-Rgt 2: 13th (self-propelled gun) Company of the SS-Panzergrenadier of the 2nd Regiment.
16. Ibid.
17. Reynolds, M., *The Devil's Adjutant,* Staplehurst, 1995, p.143.
18. For the names of tank commanders, see the beginning of Chapter 12.
19. The current road number is RN 633.
20. Sd.Kfz. 251/9: Tracked semi-armed with a 7.5-cm 24-gauge L/24 gun nicknamed Stummel (Megot) because of its short barrel.
21. Fort Leavenworth, Ike Skelton Library, AAR unit journal 119th IR December 1944.
22. Head of section.
23. De Meyer S., Haasler T., MacDougall R., Vosters S. and Weber H., *Duel in the Mist*, Newcastle, 2007, p.38.
24. Washington, NARA, Capt. Franklin Ferris, Historical Officer, 30th Infantry Division, 16-25 December 1944, p.31.
25. Berlin time was GMT+ 2.
26. Washington, NARA, *Atrocity Trial Testimony Lt Col Peiper*, Chapter IV, p.7.
27. Testimony of Strand, D., quoted in https://www.oldhickory30th.com, Accessed on 2 February 2021.
28. Testimony of Martell, C., quoted in https://www.criba.be, Accessed on 25 March 2021.
29. Wijers, H., *Die Ardennen-Offensive,* Vol 4, sl, sd, p.175.
30. Fort Leavenworth, Ike Skelton Library, *Unit Journal 119th Infantry Regiment,* December 1944.
31. Artillery tractor.
32. Washington, Library of Congress, *Veterans History Project, interview with Leon Kent*, 20 July 2003.
33. Jeanne Masson, who was present at the scene of the fighting, stated that the leather clothing of the crews came from a stock of Italian submarine equipment requisitioned during the fighting in Northern Italy.
34. De Harenne F., *Froidcour and the Two World Wars,* Froidcour, 2021, p.27.
35. Author's note: Personal knowledge.
36. Testimony of Mr Gérard Grégoire with the author.
37. S2: intelligence officer.
38. Rubel, G., *Daredevil: The Story of the 740th Tank Battalion*, sl, 1945, pp.51-60.
39. Speer, L., *110th AAA Driving Hitler's Crawlin' Coffin*, Bloomington, 2006, pp.194-5.
40. The A-2 was the second tank destroyer of Company A.
41. Fort Leavenworth, Ike Skelton Library, AAR 1-31 December, *823rd Tank Destroyer Battalion.*
42. Sherman number 10 of C Company, 743rd TB.
43. Washington, NARA, *743rd Tank Battalion S 3 journal history,* entry from 1 November – 31 December.
44. Rubel, G., *Daredevil: The Story of the 740th Tank Battalion*, sl, 1945, pp.57-8
45. Toland, J., *Bastogne*, Paris, 1962, p.132.
46. De Meyer, S. et all, *Duel in the Mist*, Vol 1, Newcastle, 2007, pp.125-52.
47. Wijers, H., *Die Ardennen-Offensive,* Vol 4, sl, sd, p.179.
48. Fort Leavenworth, Ike Skelton Library, *743rd Tank Battalion S 3 journal history from 1 November – 31 December, & 119th Unit Journal December 1944.*
49. See the photograph in *Duel in the Mist*, Newcastle, 2007, p.148.
50. Taking detours into account it is 102 kilometres from Blankeheim in Germany to Stoumont station.
51. Jentz, T., *Germany's Panther Tank,* Atglen, 1995, pp.14-18. The Panther prototype proposed by MAN, the VK3002 (M), was equipped with an AK7/200 transfer case. It was retained when it was decided to increase the tank's armour, despite the weight increase this represented.
52. See the photograph from *Duel in the Mist*, Newcastle, 2007, p.150.

Conclusion

1. MacDonald, C., *The Battle of Ardennes*, Brussels, 1984, p.380.
2. Couteau Bégarie, H., *Traité de Stratégie,* 6th ed, Paris, 2006, p.329.
3. Wenkin, H., *Blitzkrieg*, Paris, 2018, pp.262-4.

Bibliography

Archives

Washington, Library of Congress

Veterans History Project, interview with Leon Kent, 20th July 2023

Washington NARA

Administrative History Collection, G4 History, ADM No. 553, December 1944 – January 1945

Atrocity Trial Testimony Lt Col Peiper

Ferris, F., Historical Officer, 30th Infantry Division, 16-25 December 1944

Ethint interviews: 10,11,15,21,23, 25,45,50

Washington, Center of Military History, Logistics in World War II Final Report of the Army Forces

Washington, Center of Military History, The European Theater of Operations LOGISTICAL SUPPORT OF THE ARMIES, Vol I & II

After Action Report, Headquarters 30th Infantry Division

MSB 347, 733

MSC 04.24

RG407/427A/ box 19014/ folder CI 329A-14

RG407/427A/ box 19014/ folder CI 329B-14

Fort Leaveworth, Ike Skelton Library

Adams, J., *The Operations of A Company, 508th PIR (82nd Airborne Division) near Rencheux, Belgium, 22-25 December 1944 (personal experience of a Company Commander)*, Fort Benning, 1947-1948

Cain, F., *The 1111th Engineer Group in the Bulge: The Role of Engineers as Infantry in Airland Battle*, School of Advanced Military Studies, US Army Command and General Staff College, Fort Leavenworth, Kansas, 1985

Campana, V., *The Operations of the 2nd Battalion, 504th PIR (82nd Airborne Division) in the German Counter Offensive 18 December 1944 – 16 January 1945 (personal experience of a Battalion S 3)*, Fort Benning, 1946-1947

Le Febvre, H., *The Operations of the 2nd Battalion, 508th PIR (82nd Airborne Division) in the Withdrawal and the Recapture of Thier du Mont Ridge, Belgium, 22 December 1944 – 7 January 1945 (personnal experience of a Battalion operations officer)*, Fort Benning, 1948-1949

Marschall, S., *The Operations of 1st Platoon, Battery C, 80th Airborne Anti-Aircraft Battalion (82nd Airborne Division) in the Battle of the Bulge, 17 December 1944 – 3 January 1945 (personal experience of a Platoon Leader)*, Fort Benning, 1947-1948

Thompson, R.L., *The ETO Ardennes Campaign of the Combat Group Peiper, 16-26 December 1944.*

HEADQUARTERS 12 TH ARMY GROUP (FINAL AFTER ACTION REPORT), VOL II.

847-9, AAR 612th TD Battalion

8833 TD AAR 823rd TD Battaillon

847-59 AAR 825th TD Battaillon

8743 tb AAR 743rd Tank Battalion & S 3 Journal-History November – December 1944

AAR unit journal 119th I R Dec 1944

N17500-1033-2, MSB 151

N-17840, War Experiences of Commanders of German Panzer Units, General Sepp Dietrich and Colonel Joachim Peiper.
USAWC Strategy Research Project from the Red Ball Express, Carlisle Barracks Pennsylvania, US Army College

Freiburg, Bundesarchiv
MSA 873, 877, 924

Brussels, Archives of the College of Procurators General
Trial of Stavelot Goltz and others

Bastogne War Museum, Criba Fund
After Action Report, Headquarters 823rd TD Battalion
After Action Report, Headquarters 30th Infantry Division

Evere, SGRS SA
AS box, bundle 181

Memories
Blümentritt, G., *Von Rundstedt: The Soldier and the Man*, London, 1952
Burns, D., *Jump into the Valley of Shadow*, Haverton, 2011
Gavin, J., *On to Berlin*, New York, 1978
Ridgway, M., *Soldier: The Memoirs of Matthew B. Ridgway,* New York, 1956
Rubel, G., *Daredevil: The Story of the 740th Tank Battalion*, sl, 1945
Speer, A., *At the Heart of the Third Reich*, Paris, 1971
Speer, L., *110th AAA: Driving Hitler's Crawlin' Coffin,* Wroclaw, n.d
Warlimont, W., *5 ans au GQG de Hitler*, Paris, 1975

Works
War Crimes Commission, *Stavelot,* Liège, 1945
Cailloux, L., *Ardennes 1944, Pearl Harbor in Europe*, First part, Liège, 1969
Cain, F., *The 1111th Engineer Group in the Bulge: The Role of Engineers as Infantry in Airland Battle, Fort Leavenworth,* 1985
Castor, H., *La route des massacres*, Erpe, 2005
Chandler, A. et al, eds, *The Papers of Dwight David Eisenhower*, Vol IV, Baltimore – London, 1971
Cole, H., *La grande bataille des Ardennes en Belgique et au Luxembourg*, Villance-en-Ardennes, 1994
Cooke, D. and Evans, W., *Kampfgruppe Peiper at the Battle of the Bulge,* Mechanicsburgs, 2005
Couteau Bégarie, H., *Traité de Stratégie,* 6th edn, Paris, 2006
Cuppens, G., *Massacre à Malmedy*, Bayeux, 1989
De Harenne, F., *Froidcour and the Two World Wars,* Froidcour, 2021
Delaval, M., *St. Vith during Hitler's last Blitzkrieg,* Vielsalm, 1984
De Meyer S., Haasler T., MacDougall R., Vosters S. and Weber H., *Duel in the Mist*, Newcastle, 2007
Frühbeisser, R., *Opfergang deutscher Fallschirmjäger*, s.l., 1966
Götzel, H., *Generaloberst Kurt Student und seine Fallschirmjäger, die Erinnerungen des Generaloberst Kurt Student*, Friedberg, s.d., [1980]
Heptia, T., *History of the Bierset Base,* Bierset, 1990
Hewitt R., *Workhorse of the Western Front*, Washington, 1946
Jentz, T., *Germany's Panther Tank*, Atglen, 1995
Laby. H., *Ardennes 44 Stavelot,* Faimes, 1999
Liddell Hart, B.H., *Les généraux allemands parlent,* Paris, 1949
Longue, M., *Massacres en Ardennes*, Brussels, 2006

MacDonald, C., *The Battle of Ardennes*, Brussels, 1984
Merriam, R., *Dark December,* New York – Chicago, 1947
Meyer, K., *Soldier of the Reich*, Bayeux, 1996
Pergrin, D., *First Across the Rhine*, Saint-Paul, 2006
Reynolds, M., *The Devil's Adjutant,* Staplehurst, 1995
Reynolds, M., *The Devil's Warrant Officer*, Erpe, 2000
Rogister, H., *December 1944: Battle of the Bulge From Baugner to Stavelot,* CRIBA, Liège, 2009
Thayer, K., *The Young Liberators*: Vol. 2, Whitesboro, 2019
Tiemann, R., *The Leibstandarte Vol IV part 2*, Winnipeg, 1998
Toland, J., *Bastogne*, Paris, 1962
Wenkin, H., *Blitzkrieg*, Paris, 2018
Wenkin, H., *De la terreur à la Lune*, Paris-Neufchâteau, 2020.
Wenkin, H. (ed.), *Patton mis au pas*, *Mook 1944 No. 5*, Neufchâteau, 2020
Wijers, H., *The Battle of the Bulge: The Losheim Gap/Holding the Line*, Mechanicsburg, 2009
Wijers, H., *Die Ardennen-Offensive,* Vol 4, sl, sd

Webography

https://www.grenzecho.net/art/zz/reportagen/besuch-von-marlene-dietrich-in-honsfeld-in-letzter-minute-abgesagtt
http://www.criba.be
Brussels, Royal Meteorological Institute, Spa Station
Ferris, F., *The German Offensive 16 December, Defense of Spa Gas Dump,* https://www.oldhickory30th.com